616.85
c311d
2002

Carr, Alan, Dr.
Depression and
attempted suicide in
adolescence / Alan
Carr

D0942850

Depression and Attempted Suicide
in Adolescence

Parent, Adolescent and Child Training Skills 2
Series Editor: Martin Herbert

Depression and Attempted Suicide in Adolescence

by
Alan Carr

Series Editor
Martin Herbert

BPS Blackwell

616.85
C 311d
2002

© Alan Carr 2002
A BPS Blackwell book

Editorial Offices:
108 Cowley Road, Oxford OX4 1JF, UK
    Tel: +44 (0)1865 791100
350 Main Street, Malden, MA 02148-5018, USA
    Tel: +1 781 388 8250

The right of Alan Carr to be identified as the Author of this Work has been asserted in accordance with the UK Copyright, Designs and Patents Act 1988.

All rights reserved. No part of this publication may be reproduced, stored in a retrieval system, or transmitted, in any form or by any means, electronic, mechanical, photocopying, recording or otherwise, except as permitted by the UK Copyright, Designs and Patents Act 1988, without the prior permission of the publisher.

First published 2002 by The British Psychological Society and Blackwell Publishers Ltd, a Blackwell Publishing company

Library of Congress Cataloging-in-Publication Data has been applied for

ISBN 1 85433 350 X (paperback)

A catalogue record for this title is available from the British Library.

Set in Lapidary
by Ralph J. Footring, Derby
Printed and bound in Great Britain
by T J International, Padstow, Cornwall

For further information on
Blackwell Publishers, visit our website:
www.blackwellpublishers.co.uk

Contents

H F DAVIS MEMORIAL LIBRARY
COLBY COMMUNITY COLLEGE
1255 SOUTH RANGE
COLBY KS 67701

Depression and attempted suicide in adolescence

Introduction

Depression and attempted suicide are particularly serious problems in adolescence. If left untreated, they can have dire outcomes. Both depression and attempted suicide have become more common in recent times and are of central concern to professionals in the fields of health, education and social services.

Aims

The aims of this guide are to provide the practitioner with a description of depression, an explanation of factors that contribute to mood disorders and guidance on their assessment and treatment in adolescence. In addition, it aims to provide a framework for the assessment and management of adolescents who have threatened or attempted suicide.

Objectives

After studying this guide practitioners should be able to:

- describe and recognize depression in adolescence;
- answer parents' and teenagers' questions about the disorder and its consequences;
- conduct a preliminary assessment of a depressed adolescent;
- develop a formulation for an adolescent with depression;
- identify the most important targets for intervention and contribute to a treatment programme for a depressed adolescent;
- respond constructively to an adolescent who has attempted suicide or made suicidal threats and be aware of important risk factors;
- be aware of the need for liaison with colleagues in other disciplines when working with adolescents with mood disorders and at risk for suicide;
- be aware of the limitations of our knowledge base relating to adolescent depression and suicide;

➢ be aware of further readings beyond the brief account provided in this guide.

Depression in childhood or adolescence may be a particularly distressing experience for both the young person and other family members, particularly parents. Unfortunately, the outcome for depression in childhood and adolescence is not favourable. Available evidence suggests that while the majority of youngsters recover from a depressive episode within a year, they do not *grow out of* their mood disorder (Harrington, 1993; Kovacs, 1997; Reynolds and Johnson, 1994). Major depression is a recurrent condition and depressed youngsters are more likely than their non-depressed counterparts to develop episodes of depression as adults, although they are no more likely to develop other types of psychological problem. Double depression – that is an ongoing persistent mood disorder (dysthymia) and an episodic major depressive condition – severe depressive symptoms, maternal depression and the absence of conduct problems have all been shown in longitudinal studies to predict a worse outcome. While depressed youngsters with conduct difficulties have been found to be less at risk for recurrent episodes of depression, they are at greater risk for the development of relationship problems in adulthood.

Part I: Depression

Diagnostic criteria for episodes of major depression from the two most widely used classification systems for psychological problems – the DSM–IV (American Psychiatric Association, 1994) and ICD–10 (World Health Organization, 1996) – are presented in Table 1. Within DSM–IV and ICD–10, distinctions are made between:

1. major depression;
2. bipolar mood disorder;
3. dysthymia;
4. cyclothymia.

Major depression and bipolar disorder are both episodic mood disorders. The former is characterized by episodes of low mood, negative cognition, and sleep and appetite disturbance, while the latter is characterized, in addition, by episodes of mania in which elation, grandiosity, flight of ideas and expansive behaviour occur.

Dysthymia and cyclothymia are non-episodic chronic conditions. Dysthymia is characterized by depressive symptoms and cyclothymia is characterized by similar but less extreme mood fluctuations than bipolar disorder.

The distinctions between unipolar and bipolar conditions and between recurrent and persistent disorders have replaced distinctions used in earlier classifications systems. The terminology and distinctions to avoid therefore include:

➤ neurotic and psychotic depression;
➤ endogenous and reactive mood disorders;
➤ overt and masked depression.

Reviews of the classification of mood disorders (Farmer and McGuffin, 1989; Harrington, 1993) identify the following reasons for abandoning these earlier distinctions. The neurotic–psychotic distinction, based originally on inferred psychodynamic aetiological factors and differences in observable symptoms, has been discarded because the differences in psychodynamic aetiology have not been supported by empirical evidence. The endogenous–reactive distinction has been abandoned because evidence from research into the association between stressful life events and depression shows that almost all episodes of depression, regardless of quality or severity, are preceded by

Table 1. Definitions of depression, adapted from DSM–IV (American Psychiatric Association, 1994) and ICD–10 (World Health Organization, 1996)

DSM–IV criteria for a major depressive episode	*ICD–10 criteria for a depressive episode*
One or both of the following symptoms: • depressed mood (in children and adolescents can be irritable mood); • markedly diminished interest or pleasure in almost all daily activities. Three or more of the following symptoms: • significant weight loss or gain (of 5 per cent per month) or decrease/increase in appetite (in children consider failure to make expected weight gains); • insomnia or hypersomnia; • psychomotor agitation or retardation; • fatigue or loss of energy; • feelings of worthlessness, excessive guilt; • poor concentration and indecisiveness; • recurrent thoughts of death, suicidal ideation or suicide attempt. Symptoms may be reported or observed. Symptoms have been present during the same two-week period nearly every day and represent a change from previous functioning. Symptoms cause clinically significant distress or impairment in social, occupational, educational or other important areas of functioning. Symptoms are not due to a mixed episode of mania and depression. Symptoms are not due to the direct effects of a drug or a general medical conditions such as hypothyroidism. The symptoms are not better accounted for by uncomplicated bereavement.	In a typical depressive episode, the individual usually suffers from: • depressed mood; • loss of interest and enjoyment; • reduced energy; • increased fatigueability; • diminished activity; • marked tiredness after only slight effort. Other common symptoms are: • reduced concentration and attention; • reduced self-esteem and confidence; • ideas of guilt and unworthiness; • bleak and pessimistic views of the future; • ideas or acts of self-harm or suicide; • disturbed sleep; • diminished appetite. Some of the above symptoms may be marked and develop characteristic features that are widely regarded as having special significance, for example the *somatic symptoms* that are listed below: • loss of interest or pleasure in activities that are normally enjoyable; • lack of emotional reactivity to normally pleasurable surroundings; • waking in the morning two hours or more before the usual time; • depression worse in the mornings; • psychomotor retardation or agitation; • marked loss of appetite or weight; • marked loss of libido. Usually the somatic syndrome is not regarded as present unless at least four of these symptoms are present. A duration of two weeks is required for a diagnosis of depression. The lowered mood varies little from day to day and is often unresponsive to circumstances and may show a characteristic diurnal variation as the day goes on. *Atypical presentations* are particularly common in adolescence. In some cases anxiety, distress and motor agitation may be more prominent at times than depression, and mood changes may be masked by such features as irritability, excessive consumption of alcohol, histrionic behaviour and exacerbation of pre-existing phobic or obsessional symptoms or by hypochondriacal preoccupations.

stressful life events and in that sense are reactive. The recognition that youngsters with depression may also show conduct disorders has rendered the concept of masked depression unnecessary, since the term was often used to classify depressed youngsters who *masked* their low mood with angry outbursts of aggressive or destructive behaviour.

Epidemiology of depression

Depression is not a rare condition and is more prevalent among adolescents than children (Harrington, 1993). In community samples, prevalence rates of depression in pre-adolescence range from 0.5 per cent to 2.5 per cent and in adolescents from 2 per cent to 8 per cent. Depression is very common among clinic referrals: in clinic studies of children and adolescents, about 25 per cent of referrals are depressed.

Depression quite commonly occurs in conjunction with other disorders, particularly in children referred for treatment. In community studies of childhood depression, co-morbidity rates of 10–17 per cent have been found for conduct disorder, anxiety disorders and attention deficit disorder (Carr, 1999).

Sex differences in the distribution of depression have consistently been found. Depression is equally common in pre-adolescent boys and girls but more common in adolescent girls than boys (Cohen *et al.*, 1993). This greater preponderance of depression among teenage girls compared with boys is similar to the sex distribution of depression among adults. The relative contribution of biological factors and psychosocial factors to this sex difference in prevalence is currently unclear. It is possible that the differential impact of hormonal changes in puberty on boys and girls and differing role demands on male and female adolescents contribute to more adolescent girls developing depression.

Clinical features of depression

The main features of depression are presented in Table 2 (Harrington, 1993; Kovacs, 1997; Reynolds and Johnson, 1994). These features may be linked by assuming that the depressed youngster has usually suffered a loss of some sort – loss of an important relationship, loss of some valued attribute such as athletic ability or health, or loss of status.

With respect to affect, low mood is a core feature of depression. Depressed mood is usually reported as a feeling of sadness, loneliness or despair and an

Table 2. Clinical features of depression in children and adolescents

Domain	Clinical features
Mood	Depressed mood Inability to experience pleasure Irritable mood Anxiety and apprehension
Behaviour	Psychomotor retardation or agitation Depressive stupor*
Relationships	Deterioration in family relationships Withdrawal from peer relationships Poor school performance
Somatic state	Fatigue Disturbance of sleep Aches and pains Loss of appetite or overeating Change in weight* Diurnal variation of mood (worse in morning) Loss of interest in sex
Cognition	Negative view of self, world and future Excessive guilt Suicidal ideation* Mood-congruent delusions* Cognitive distortions Inability to concentrate Indecision
Perception	Perceptual bias towards negative events Mood-congruent hallucinations*

*These features occur in severe episodes of depression.

inability to experience pleasure. Alternatively, irritability, anxiety and aggression may be the main features, with sadness and inability to experience pleasure being less prominent. Depressed children and adolescents may show some cocktail of all three emotional processes, that is depressed mood, irritability and anxiety.

At a behavioural level, depressed youngsters may show either reduced and slowed activity levels (psychomotor retardation) or increased but ineffective activity (psychomotor agitation). They may show a failure to engage in activities that would bring them a sense of achievement or connectedness to family or friends. Where youngsters become immobile, this is referred to as depressive stupor. Fortunately, this is rare.

At an interpersonal level, depressed children report a deterioration in their relationships with family, friends, teachers and other significant figures in their lives. They describe themselves as lonely and yet unable or unworthy of taking steps to make contact with others.

Somatic or vegetative features associated with more severe conditions include the following:

- loss of energy;
- disturbances of sleep and appetite;
- weight loss or failure to make age-appropriate weight gain;
- abdominal pains or headaches;
- diurnal variation in mood.

Teenagers may also report losing interest in sex. These features of depression are consistent with findings that dysregulation of neurophysiological, endocrine and immune functions are associated with depression and that sleep architecture is also affected.

With respect to cognition, depressed children describe themselves, the world and the future in negative terms. They evaluate themselves as worthless and are critical of their academic, athletic, musical and social accomplishments. Often this negative self-evaluation is expressed as guilt for not living up to certain standards or for letting others down. They see their world, including family, friends and school, as unrewarding, critical and hostile or apathetic. They describe the future in bleak terms and report little, if any, hope that things will improve.

Where they report extreme hopelessness coupled with excessive guilt for actions that they believe deserve punishment, suicidal ideas or intentions may be reported. Suicide will be discussed in detail Part II of this guide.

Extremely negative thoughts about the self, the world and the future may be woven together in severe cases into depressive delusional systems. In addition to the content of depressed youngsters' thoughts being bleak, they also display logical errors in their thinking and concentration problems. Errors in reasoning are marked by a tendency to maximize the significance and implications of negative events and minimize the significance of positive events. Concentration and attention difficulties lead to difficulties with schoolwork or leisure activities demanding sustained attention.

With respect to perception, having suffered a loss, depressed children tend to perceive the world as if further losses were probable. Depressed children selectively attend to negative features of the environment and this in turn leads them to engage in depressive cognitions and unrewarding behaviour patterns, which further entrenches their depressed mood. In severe cases of adolescent depression, youngsters may report mood-congruent auditory hallucinations. We may assume that this severe perceptual abnormality is present when youngsters report hearing voices criticizing them or telling them depressive things. Auditory hallucinations also occur in schizophrenia. However, the hallucinations that occur in schizophrenia are not necessarily mood-congruent.

Assessment of depression

In the management of mood problems, the first priority is to assess the risk of self-harm. A structured approach to the assessment and formulation of suicide risk is presented in Part II of this guide. Once suicide risk has been managed, it is appropriate to begin a more thorough assessment of the mood disorder.

A second priority is to determine whether the depression is a response to child abuse, which requires a child protection intervention. To evaluate this possibility, it is essential at some point to interview adolescents alone and ask whether, currently, anyone is hurting them, bullying them, or treating them in a way that makes them unhappy. Where adolescents are exposed regularly to physical, sexual, or emotional abuse or neglect, the offer of treatment outside of a statutory child-protection framework may reinforce the pattern of abuse. So, if adolescent depression reflects a response to ongoing abuse or neglect, then a child-protection intervention is essential before proceeding to treat the depression.

The third priority when children or adolescents present with a mood disorder is to clarify the nature and extent of the symptoms. The clinical features in Tables 1 and 2 offer a useful basis for interviewing in this area. Self-report questionnaires and rating scales that may supplement clinical interviewing are contained Appendices 1, 7 and 8. The important questions to ask when assessing a depressed youngster are outlined in the next section.

The fourth priority is to identify any predisposing, precipitating, maintaining and protective factors associated with the youngster's depression. An outline of important areas to cover in such interviews is given below. The questions are based on the theoretical positions outlined above and also on the empirical and clinical literature on depression in adolescence (Asarnow *et al.*, 1993; Harrington, 1993; Mufson *et al.*, 1993; Oster and Caro, 1990; Reynolds and Johnson, 1994; Stark and Kendall, 1996).

In assessing a youngster with depression, it is useful to begin by interviewing the parents and the youngster together, and enquire about the symptoms as well as predisposing, precipitating, maintaining and protective factors in that meeting. This may be followed immediately by separate interviews with the parents and the adolescent in which they are given the opportunity to say things about the problem, and factors that cause and maintain it, that they might not feel free to say in the joint family interview.

If an incomplete picture emerges from these interviews, it may be helpful to arrange to interview other family members, school staff and significant members of the adolescent's network.

Assessing symptoms

Enquiries about symptoms should invite family members to comment on the areas listed in Tables 1 and 2. Here are some questions that may be useful in this regard.

General questions about the presenting problem

It is most useful to begin with a broad general enquiry, such as:

➤ What is your main concern about yourself (your youngster)?

You may follow up this and all subsequent specific questions with probes, such as:

➤ Can you give an example of that?

   Or:

➤ Can you say a little more about that?

These questions may be followed by more specific enquiries about mood, behaviour, relationships, somatic state, cognition and perception if necessary.

Questions about mood

➤ How has your (your youngster's) mood been recently?
➤ Have you (has your youngster) been more sad than usual or about the same?
➤ Have you (has your youngster) been more irritable or annoyed than usual or about the same?
➤ Have you (has your youngster) been more anxious or uptight than usual or about the same?
➤ Have you (has your youngster) been enjoying yourself (him/herself) less than usual or about the same?

Questions about behaviour

➤ How has your (your youngster's) behaviour been recently?
➤ Have you (has your youngster) been doing fewer things than usual or about the same?

Questions about relationships

➢ How have your (has your youngster's) relationships at home and at school been recently?
➢ Are they more problematic than usual or the same as usual?

Questions about somatic state

➢ Have you (has your youngster) been sleeping okay recently?
➢ Has your (your youngster's) appetite or weight changed lately?
➢ Has your (your youngster's) mood been better in the morning or the evening?
➢ Have you noticed any change in your interest in sex recently?

Questions about cognition

➢ How do you (does your youngster) see yourself (him/herself) and the direction your (his/her) life is taking at present?
➢ How proud are you (is your youngster) of your (his/her) achievements?
➢ Can you tell me about your (your youngster's) plans for the future?
➢ Are you (is your youngster) able to concentrate as well now as you (he/she) ever were?
➢ Have you (has your youngster) had more difficulty making decisions recently?

Questions about perception

➢ Have you ever noticed that you were being told bad things about yourself and found that you could not see who was saying these things?

Information about symptoms from an assessment interview may be supplemented with information from the mood questionnaire contained in Appendix 1.

Assessing predisposing factors

Not all adolescents who experience losses develop clinical depression. Those youngsters who do develop a mood disorder typically have been rendered vulnerable to depression by biological factors or early life experiences. Among the more important predisposing risk factors for mood disorders are:

➢ a genetic vulnerability, as indicated by a family history of mood disorders;

➤ early experiences of loss;
➤ problematic parenting;
➤ personal characteristics and traits.

Loss experiences may include health-related losses such as difficulties associated with pre- or perinatal complications and early illness or injury. Psychosocial losses may include bereavements, separations, institutional care, social disadvantage and loss of trusting relationships through abuse.

Problematic parenting styles may lead to children having difficulty developing secure attachments to parents, and consequently they may not develop secure internal working models for close relationships in later life. This deficit may make them vulnerable to depression. A punitive, critical and authoritarian parenting style, where the parent focuses on the children's failures rather than successes, may render them vulnerable to depression. These children, as a result of such parenting, may be sensitized to experiences of failure and threats to their autonomy. Neglectful parenting, on the other hand, may sensitize the child to loss of relationships and threats of abandonment. Parental depression or drug or alcohol abuse may subserve these problematic parenting styles. Marital discord and family disorganization may also create a context in which these types of non-optimal parenting occur.

Personal characteristics of the adolescent such as low intelligence, difficult or inhibited temperament, low self-esteem and an external locus of control may predispose adolescents to developing depression. Low intelligence may be associated with failure to achieve valued academic goals. Difficult or inhibited temperament may compromise the youngster's capacity to regulate mood and this in turn may interfere with the development of supportive relationships. Negative self-evaluative beliefs and the belief that important sources of reinforcement are beyond personal control may render youngsters vulnerable to self-criticism and helplessness, which are part of the depressive experience.

Questions about predisposing factors

➤ Has anyone in your family had problems with low mood or depression?
➤ At birth, during infancy or childhood did you (your youngster) have any health problems?
➤ Did you (your youngster) have any major losses or separations during childhood?
➤ Were both of your parents (you) in good health and without major problems during your (your youngster's) childhood?
➤ What kind of relationship did you have with your parents (your youngster) during your (his/her) childhood?

> ➤ How did you (your youngster) fare at school during your (his/her) child-hood?
> ➤ To what extent did you (your youngster) feel like you were (he/she was) in control of your (his/her) life during childhood?
> ➤ To what extent were you (your youngster) happy with yourself (him/herself) and your (his/her) situation during your (his/her) childhood?

Assessing precipitating factors

Experiences of loss associated with the disruption of significant relationships and those associated with failure to achieve valued goals, and therefore threats to autonomy, may precipitate an episode of depression in adolescence. Relationships may be disrupted through illness, parent–child separations, parental divorce, moving house, moving school, bullying or abuse. Failure to achieve valued goals may occur with failure in examinations, and illnesses or injuries that prevent success in sports or leisure activities.

Questions about precipitating factors

Here are some questions that may throw light on possible precipitating factors:

> ➤ What events, in your opinion, led to the current problems you have described?
> ➤ Have there been major illnesses or losses within the family recently?
> ➤ Have there been changes in the home or school recently that have been particularly difficult?
> ➤ Have you (your youngster) experienced any major disappointments recently?

Assessing maintaining factors

Not all vulnerable adolescents who experience losses develop clinical depression. In order for a vulnerable youngster to develop a mood disorder, typically they must find themselves in a situation where either personal or contextual factors, or both, maintain their depressive symptoms.

Personal cognitive factors that maintain low mood include negative automatic thoughts and cognitive distortions that arise from negative cognitive schemas. These have been outlined in Beck's (1976) cognitive theory of depression. According to Beck's theory, depression occurs when life events involving loss occur and reactivate negative cognitive schemas formed in childhood as a result of early loss experiences. These negative schemas entail negative assumptions such as 'If I am not liked by everybody, then I am worthless'. When activated, such schemas underpin the occurrence of negative automatic thoughts, such as 'No one here likes me', and cognitive distortions, such as *all-or-nothing thinking*.

According to Beck, two negative schemas that contain latent attitudes about the self, the world and the future are of particular importance in depression. The first relates to interpersonal relationships and the second to personal achievement. He referred to these as sociotropy and autonomy. Individuals who have negative self-schemas in which sociotropy is the central organizing theme define themselves negatively if they perceive themselves to be failing in maintaining positive relationships. Thus their core assumption about the self may be 'If I am not liked by everybody, then I am worthless'. Individuals who have negative self-schemas in which autonomy is the central organizing theme define themselves negatively if they perceive themselves to be failing in achieving work-related goals. Thus their core assumption about the self may be 'If I am not a success and in control, then I am worthless'.

When faced with life stresses, individuals vulnerable to depression because of early experience of loss and the related development of negative self-schemas become prone to interpreting ambiguous situations in negative, mood-depressing ways. The various logical errors that they make are referred to by Beck as cognitive distortions and these include the following:

➢ *all-or-nothing thinking* – thinking in extreme categorical terms, for example 'I'm either a success or a failure';

➢ *selective abstraction* – selectively focusing on a small aspect of a situation and drawing conclusions from this, for example 'I made a mistake so every thing I did was wrong';

➢ *overgeneralization* – generalizing from one instance to all possible in-stances, for example 'He didn't say hello so he must hate me';

➢ *magnification* – exaggerating the significance of an event, for example 'She said there were two errors in my work. That means my whole project is worthless';

➢ *personalization* – attributing negative feeling of others to the self, for example 'He looked really angry when he walked into the room, so I must have done something wrong';

➢ *emotional reasoning* – taking feelings as facts, for example 'I feel like the future is black so the future is hopeless'.

Depressed individuals interpret situations in terms of their negative cognitive schemas and so their automatic thoughts are characterized by these depressive cognitive distortions. Automatic thoughts are self-statements that occur without apparent volition when an individual attempts to interpret a situation so as to respond to it in a coherent way.

A depressive attributional style, where internal, global, stable attributions are made for failure experiences, and external, specific, unstable attributions are made for success, can also maintain depression (Abramson *et al.*, 1978).

Low mood may be maintained by high levels of self-criticism and low self-efficacy beliefs. Self-efficacy beliefs are beliefs about the extent to which one has the ability to change one's behaviour effectively, to achieve specific goals. Other important cognitive factors that maintain depression include selectively monitoring negative aspects of one's actions, engaging in high levels of punitive self-talk or punishment; and engaging in little positive self-talk or self-reinforcement. Self-defeating behavioural patterns that arise from social skills deficits, particularly engaging others in depressive conversations, which lead them to avoid future interactions, may maintain depressed mood. Depression may be maintained or exacerbated by using dysfunctional coping strategies, particularly substance abuse and self-harming gestures.

Immature defences for dealing with perceived threats, such as denial, projection or reaction formation, may also maintain depressed mood (Bateman *et al.*, 2000). With denial, youngsters deny their problems or their capacity to solve them rather than realistically dealing with them. With projection, they attribute their own deficits to others rather than themselves. With reaction formation, they treat people towards whom they feel aggression with excessive deference. All of these immature defences lead to the maintenance rather than the resolution of stressful relationships, which in turn maintain depression.

At a biological level, depression may be maintained by dysregulation of the amine system governing reward and punishment processes; dysregulation of the endocrine system and the immune system governing defence against illness; and desynchrony of the sleep–waking cycle (Reynolds and Johnson, 1994).

Within the youngster's family or school context a variety of factors may maintain mood problems (Carr, 2000). These include ongoing inescapable abuse, bullying or punishment in the absence of adequate support or being in an unsupportive educational placement. Ongoing interactions with parents or primary carers characterized by excessive criticism, neglect or excessive overinvolvement may maintain depression, as may family circumstances where the youngster is blocked from achieving developmental tasks such as establishing autonomy. These parenting patterns may be subserved by confused family communication, family disorganization, and *triangulation*, where the depressed youngster is caught between conflicting parental demands. These types of difficulty may arise in family contexts where parents have high levels of stress, including: social disadvantage; low levels of social support; marital discord; low father involvement; physical illness; or psychological problems, including depression. Where parents have insecure internal working models for relationships, low self-esteem, low self-efficacy, an external locus of control, immature defences and poor coping strategies, their re-sourcefulness in managing their child's depression may be compromised. Parents may also become involved in problem-maintaining interactions with their children if they have inaccurate knowledge about the role of psychological factors in the genesis and maintenance of depression.

Within the treatment system, a lack of coordination and clear communication among the professionals involved, including family physicians, paediatricians, nurses, teachers and psychologists, may maintain an adolescent's depression. It is not unusual for various members of the professional network to offer conflicting opinions and advice on the nature and management adolescent depression. These may range from viewing the child as psychiatrically ill and deserving inpatient care, antidepressant medication and permissive management, to seeing the child as delinquent and requiring strict behavioural control. Where problems with cooperation between families and treatment teams develop, and families deny the existence of the problems, the validity of the diagnosis and the formulation or the appropriateness of the treatment programme, then the adolescent's difficulties may persist. Parents' lack of experience in dealing with similar problems in the past is a further factor that may compromise their capacity to work cooperatively with the treatment team and so may contribute to the maintenance of the adolescent's difficulties.

Assessing protective factors

The probability that a treatment programme will be effective is influenced by a variety of personal and contextual protective factors. It is important that these be assessed and included in the later formulation, since it is protective factors that usually serve as the foundation for therapeutic change. Youngsters with less severe mood disorders that are clearly episodic and who also have conduct problems are less at risk than those with double depression (severe episodic mood disorder superimposed on a persistent milder mood problem) and no conduct problems. At a biological level, physical fitness and a willingness to engage in regular physical exercise are protective factors. A high IQ, an easy temperament, high self-esteem, an internal locus of control, high self-efficacy and an optimistic attributional style are all important personal protective factors. Other important personal protective factors include mature defence mechanisms and functional coping strategies, particularly good problem-solving skills and a capacity to make and maintain friendships.

Within the family, secure parent–child attachment and authoritative parenting are central protective factors, particularly if they occur within the context of a flexible family structure in which there is clear communication, high marital satisfaction and the parents share the day-to-day tasks of managing home life.

Good parental adjustment is also a protective factor. Where parents have an internal locus of control, high self-efficacy, high self-esteem, internal working models for secure attachments, an optimistic attributional style, mature defences and functional coping strategies, then they are better re-sourced to manage their child's difficulties constructively. Parents' accurate knowledge about the role of psychological factors in recovery from depression is also a protective factor.

Within the broader social network, high levels of support, low levels of stress and membership of a high socio-economic group are all protective factors for depressed adolescents. Where families are embedded in social networks that provide a high level of support and place few stressful demands on family members, then it is less likely that parents' and children's resources for dealing with health-related problems will become depleted. A well resourced educational placement may also be viewed as a protective factor. Educational placements where teachers have sufficient time and flexibility to attend home–school liaison meetings if invited to do so may contribute to positive outcomes for depressed adolescents.

Within the treatment system, cooperative working relationships between the treatment team and the family and good coordination of multi-professional input are protective factors. Families are more likely to benefit from treatment when they accept the formulation of the problem given by the treatment team and are committed to working with the team to resolve it. Where families have successfully faced similar problems before, then they are more likely to benefit from treatment and in this sense previous experi-ence with similar problems is a protective factor.

Questions about maintaining and protective factors

➤ When you try to do something (at home or school or with friends) and fail to do it right, what do you think or say to yourself (inside your head)?
➤ Which do you (does your youngster) notice more: the things you do (your youngster does) right or the things you do (your youngster does) wrong?
➤ How do you (does your youngster) go about joining in with other young-sters who are doing something that interests you (him/her)?
➤ How do you (does your youngster) cope when things don't go the way you want (your youngster wants) them to?
➤ Do you (does your youngster) usually think that things are going to turn out well or badly?
➤ How have your parents been supporting you since you have developed a low mood?

➤ Are you (is your youngster) usually clear on what your parents (you both) think about your (his/her) situation?

➤ Are your parents (you both) in good health at the moment?

➤ Have your parents (you both) any major problems that affect you (your youngster) at the moment?

➤ Are you (is your youngster) happy with your (his/her) school situation at the moment?

➤ Do you (does your youngster) think that all the people that are trying to help with your (his/her) problems at present are like a team or are they all disagreeing with each other or not talking to each other about the right thing to do?

Formulation

For convenience, lists of possible predisposing, precipitating, maintaining and protective factors to consider in the assessment of depression are given in Figure 1. Following thorough assessment interviews, a case formulation may be drawn up. This formulation should:

➤ link predisposing, precipitating, maintaining and protective factors to the depressive symptoms;

➤ suggest treatment goals;

➤ outline plans for reaching these goals.

Here is an example of a formulation for a teenager who was referred for treatment of depression and school-based conduct problems:

> Alice shows affective, cognitive, behavioural and somatic features consistent with a diagnosis of depression. The current episode has lasted about a year. In addition, she shows a variety of conduct problems, which began in early adolescence and have fluctuated since.
>
> Predisposing factors for her mood disorder include a probable genetic predisposition and an early separation experience during her mother's postpartum depression.
>
> The current episode was precipitated by the move to Arklow, which involved the loss of important friendships and the loss of a school context in which she was accepted and was performing above average.
>
> Her depressed state is maintained by her self-defeating cognitive style, the fact that she has now resigned herself to an isolated position in her new school, and the fact that she and her parents have developed a style of interacting that is either critical or overinvolved.
>
> These immediate maintaining factors occur within a wider social context where both her parents find themselves virtually unsupported and under high levels of stress. For Alice's father the main stresses are work-related and for

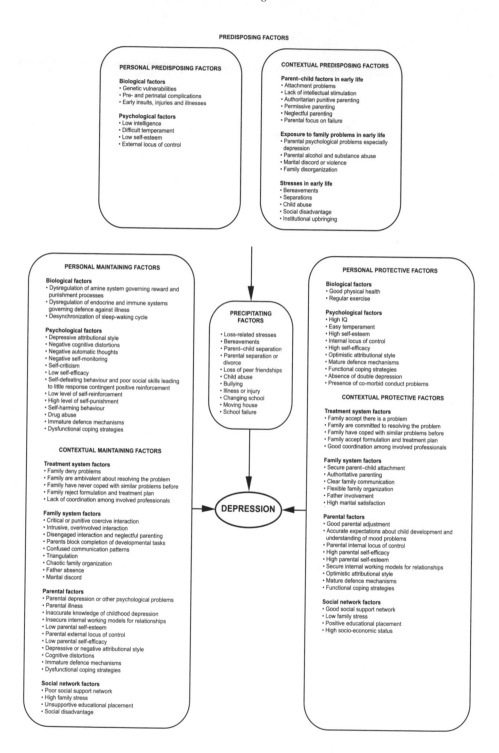

Figure 1. Factors to consider in the assessment of depression.

Alice's mother, isolation is the main source of stress. The high stress and low support have begun to erode the good working relationship that Alice's mother and father enjoyed as parents and marital partners before the move to Arklow.

Alice's conduct problems (verbal aggression, defiance and rule breaking at school) appear to be secondary to the depression. They reflect an attempt to cope with isolation by mixing with deviant peers.

There are a number of important protective factors in this case, which suggest that there may be a positive outcome. These include Alice's high overall level of academic ability and problem-solving skills; her ability in the past to make and maintain friendships; the parents' demonstrated capacity to maintain a good marital relationship over many years and in the face of the mother's three major episodes of depression; and the parents' and Alice's commitment to resolving the problem.

Treatment in this case involved family work to improve the level of support offered to Alice by her parents; liaison with the school, which aimed to increase Alice's involvement in structured activities such as sports and drama; and individual cognitive therapy work, which aimed to help Alice challenge her negative beliefs and improve her problem-solving skills.

Treatment of depression

Thorough assessment typically reveals that the youngster's mood problems are maintained by personal factors, family-based factors, school-based factors and possibly factors within the child's wider network. While it is useful for the core intervention to target the child and family, interventions with the school or ward staff in hospitalized cases, or focusing on the parents in multiproblem families, may be necessary.

In the treatment protocol given here, I have attempted to integrate those techniques that have been shown to be effective in the cognitive behavioural literature with well established systemic, interpersonal and social-learning approaches to working with families (Oster and Caro, 1990; Carr, 2000; Kaslow and Rehm, 1991; Lewinsohn *et al.*, 1994; Mufson *et al.*, 1993; Williams, 1992). The following elements are contained in this approach to treatment:

> ➤ psychoeducation;
> ➤ self-monitoring;
> ➤ interventions focusing on activity;
> ➤ interventions focusing on family relationships;
> ➤ interventions focusing on cognition;
> ➤ training in social skills and problem-solving;

> ➤ school interventions;
> ➤ medication;
> ➤ management of parental mood problems;
> ➤ management of relapse, disengagement and resistance.

Psychoeducation

Psychoeducational input is appropriately offered early in the consultation process so that the adolescent and family can have a common understanding of depression with the treatment team. However, throughout therapy it is necessary to remind clients from time to time about various aspects of this way of conceptualizing depression. Depression is explained as a complex condition involving changes in mood, biological functioning, thinking, behaviour and relationships. Vulnerability to depression may be due to genetic factors or early loss experiences. Current episodes of depression arise from a build-up of recent life stress. This activates the vulnerability, which then comes to be maintained by depressed thinking, action and relationships. Genetic vulnerability may be explained as a nervous system that *goes slow* under pressure and disrupts sleep, appetite and energy. This going slow leads to depressed mood. Early loss-related vulnerability may be explained as a set of memories about loss that have been filed away, but are taken out when a recent loss occurs. The files inform the youngster that more and more losses will occur and this leads to depressed mood. Treatment centres on helping youngsters and their families learn how to control and change patterns of thinking, action and relationships that maintain depression.

It is important to highlight that the youngster's thinking processes or beliefs, behavioural routines and ways of managing relationships that maintain depressed mood are under conscious control, so treatment will focus on coaching the youngster to change these three things. The role of the family is to help the youngster develop new beliefs, routines and ways of managing relationships that protect him or her from becoming stuck in low moods. Within this context, protective factors, particularly social support from the family, may be mentioned. This allows the youngster and the family to view themselves as a problem-solving team. A diagram and some notes about this explanation of depression is presented in Appendix 2 and may be photocopied and given to clients as part of the psychoeducational input.

Somatic state has also been included in the model. It can be mentioned that antidepressant medication may be used to regulate sleep and appetite and increase energy levels. The results of treatment trials show that selective serotonin reuptake inhibitors but not tricyclic antidepressants are more effective than placebos in the treatment of adolescents with depression (Riddle *et al.*, 2001).

If parents or youngsters are unable to understand this model of mood problems, repeatedly trying to enlighten them, in my experience, evokes resistance rather than cooperation. In these cases, it may be best to offer a very simple programme that has demonstrated effectiveness, that is relaxation training over eight sessions (Wood *et al.*, 1996).

If parents understand the model but disagree with it, repeated argument is even more unlikely to lead to acceptance. This typically occurs in families where a parent or other family member has been treated with antidepressants for a mood disorder and believes that the same treatment is the most appropriate for their teenager. Our primary responsibility in such cases is to let parents know that the evidence for the efficacy of antidepressants with adolescents is not great and that little is known about possible long-term adverse effects. Good practice is to resort to antidepressants only in instances where psychological interventions have not been effective.

Self-monitoring

Self-monitoring and goal setting may be introduced together in the earliest stages of therapy. The youngster and the family are invited to set very small achievable goals, which, if reached, would clearly demonstrate that improvement was occurring. An example of such a goal would be having at least one period in the day when the youngster's mood rises at least 1 point on a 10-point scale or having three periods of a half day in a week when a mood rating of at least 5 points was achieved. The idea of tracking progress towards these mood change goals by keeping a diary may be introduced at this point. It is best at this early stage to invite the adolescent to keep a simple type of diary, which should be completed each time the youngster notices a significant change in mood. The diary may be organized as four columns with the following headings:

➤ the date and time of the entry;
➤ the activity that led to the change in mood rating;
➤ a mood rating on a 10-point scale before the activity;
➤ a mood rating on a 10-point scale after the activity.

This type of diary helps adolescents and parents develop an awareness of the link between activity and mood. The diary should be reviewed in each session and links made between carrying out particular activities or engaging in particular types of relationships and mood. Youngsters may find from this type of diary that particular types of events are associated with higher moods. Such events may include physical activity, manageable challenges, cooperative activities in positive relationships with others, particular types of low-key conversations and so forth. They may also identify events and types of relationships that lower mood, such as inactivity, watching television, solitary playing of videogames, critical and conflictual relationships with others and so forth.

This type of self-monitoring provides a basis for introducing a number of interventions based on scheduling activities associated with higher moods. These may include graded tasks, physical exercise, pleasant events and age-appropriate challenges. Another intervention that should be scheduled is relaxation training. All of these are discussed below. The youngster may be invited to complete one or more of these types of task both in the session and between sessions and note their impact on mood in the diary.

Reviews of this type of diary also allow teenagers and their parents to track the relationship between mood and certain types of social interaction that commonly occur within the family or peer group. It is not unusual for parents to learn that conversations intended to cheer their child up actually depressed the youngster further, whereas fairly neutral exchanges led to improvements in mood. Family members may also become aware of the negative impact of family conflict on the teenager by reviewing four-column diaries. This type of information provides a basis for relationship-focused interventions, including family communication training; family problem-solving training; providing support; and renegotiating role relationships. The impact of using these skills in family conversations on the youngster's mood may be tested in treatment sessions and also between sessions and the results noted in the diary.

Later, a new column may be added to the diary, in which youngsters record the *thoughts* or ideas that went through their minds and which contributed to their mood rating. Training in capturing negative automatic thoughts and understanding cognitive distortions should precede this self-monitoring assignment and this is discussed below. In this type of self-monitoring task the following five columns should be included in the diary:

➢ the date and time of the entry;
➢ the activity that led to the change in mood rating;
➢ a mood rating on a 10-point scale before the activity;
➢ the thoughts that the person had about the activity or relationship that contributed to the mood rating;
➢ a mood rating on a 10-point scale after the activity.

Reviewing this type of diary allows the adolescent and family members to see that the youngster's interpretation of events contributes to negative mood. This provides a rationale for teaching the *challenge*, *test*, *reward* (CTR) routine for challenging negative automatic thoughts, described below. Conducting this type of training in family sessions is particularly important in families where a parent suffers from depression, since it provides such parents with a strategy for being less critical of their depressed child. Many depressed parents attribute negative intentions and qualities to their children, who subsequently develop depression, and unless this process can be modified, youngsters may find that it contributes to relapses.

Once youngsters have become proficient in using diaries that allow the impact of activities, relationships and thoughts on mood to be tracked, two additional columns may be added, in which coping strategies used to alter mood and the impact of these on mood are noted. A full seven-column diary form is presented in Appendix 3. This diary page may be copied and enlarged with a photocopier for use with clients. It may also be modified by covering unwanted columns to yield four- and five-column diary pages.

Interventions focusing on activity

Through psychoeducation and diary keeping, adolescents and their families discover that activity directly affects mood. Small tasks, pleasant tasks and age-appropriate challenges all improve mood, whereas large tasks, unpleasant events and being blocked from facing age-appropriate challenges lead to a depressed mood. Physical exercise and relaxation also promote a positive mood. In light of this, there are certain interventions that help youngsters develop activity patterns that improve mood. These include:

➢ scheduling graded tasks;
➢ scheduling pleasant events;
➢ remembering pleasant events;
➢ scheduling age-appropriate challenges;
➢ scheduling physical exercise;
➢ using relaxation skills.

Scheduling graded tasks

Depressed youngsters may report that there are things that they feel they should do or want to do but believe that they cannot because the tasks appear to be overwhelming. In scheduling graded tasks, the youngster is invited to break seemingly insuperable tasks into small manageable tasks, complete these and receive reinforcement for doing so (Beck, 1976). Parents and youngsters may be invited to work together in a treatment session and break a big task into smaller tasks and agree on a reward system using points, whereby the adolescent will be reinforced or rewarded for completing each small component of the large task. The number of points that may be earned for completing each small task must be clearly agreed. The way in which points will be given and the place where they will be stored must all be carefully agreed in treatment sessions. A menu of prizes or privileges that the youngster really wants to obtain and which may be bought for a specified number of points must be agreed with the youngster and parents before implementing a reward system like this.

Reward systems rarely work without some minor difficulties that require fine-tuning. If the tasks are too large and so not completed, make them smaller. If points are not dispensed fairly soon after successful task completion, the youngster may abandon the system. In these instances arrange for more immediate delivery of points after task completion. If youngsters do not seem bothered about obtaining items from the menu of prizes and privileges, reformulate the menu with them so that it contains highly valued items. If youngsters earn points but do not cash them in for items from the menu, then organize an easier way for exchanging points for prizes and privileges.

Scheduling pleasant events

Parents and youngsters may be invited to draw up lists of pleasant events, such as going for a walk together or watching a film, which the adolescent believes are associated with improved mood, and plan to carry these out (Lewinsohn *et al.*, 1994).

Remembering pleasant events

Parents may be shown how to schedule a period each evening to help youngsters review their day and remember all the positive things that have happened, list these and post them on the fridge door or the child's bedroom wall (Williams, 1992).

Scheduling age appropriate challenges

Where adolescents and their parents have become entrenched in patterns of interaction appropriate to the pre-adolescent stage of development, families may be invited to arrange for adolescents to work gradually towards dealing with age-appropriate challenges. These may include travelling independently to meet with friends, shopping for their own clothes, planning to stay overnight at a friend's house and so forth.

Scheduling physical exercise

Youngsters and their parents may be invited gradually to increase the amount of daily physical exercise the teenager takes, since inactivity maintains low mood, and regular exercise, particularly aerobic exercise, improves mood.

Using relaxation skills

Youngsters may be trained either directly or through their parents in using relaxation, breathing and visualization skills. A set of such exercises is given in Appendix 4. These skills are particularly useful where the youngster experiences irritability and anxiety as part of the mood disorder. They may also be used with sleep problems. Youngsters may be invited to practise relaxation exercises at bedtime to facilitate sleep onset.

When coaching parents in relaxation instruction, model the process first by going through the exercises listed in Appendix 4 with the youngster while the parents observe. Use a slow, calming tone of voice and repetition of instructions as required to help the youngster achieve a relaxed state. Before and after the exercises check with the youngster how relaxed he or she feels on a 10-point scale, where 1 reflects complete relaxation and 10 reflects extreme anxiety. Most adolescents will report that, even on their first trial, they achieve some tension reduction. This should be praised and interpreted to the youngster and the parents as an indication that the adolescent has the aptitude for developing and refining his/her relaxation skills. The parents may then be invited to instruct the youngster in completing the exercises daily and to praise the adolescent for completing the exercises.

For a minority of youngsters, the relaxation exercises lead to increased tension. This may occur because the adolescent is made aware, by completing the exercises, of body tension that is normally ignored. Alternatively, it may occur because focusing attention on somatic processes during the exercises induces anxiety. In such instances, work on only one or two muscle groups at a time and keep the training periods very short. Also request regular anxiety ratings from the adolescent and, when increases in anxiety occur, provide a distraction by asking him or her to engage in the visualization exercise described in Appendix 4.

With some such youngsters, it may be necessary to abandon the muscle relaxation exercises completely and concentrate on training them in visualization or focusing on an external, repetitive, calming visual or auditory stimulus as a means of attaining a relaxed state. (For some of my clients I have used such stimuli as music, candlelight, and a bowl of goldfish!) The important thing is to find a routine that the adolescent can reliably use to reduce the subjective sense of anxiety, as indicated by the rating on the 10-point anxiety scale. Some youngsters find the scene described for the visualization exercise given in Appendix 4 is not relaxing. In such instances, ask the adolescent to describe an alternative relaxing scene, such as being in a wood or on top of a mountain, and use this as an alternative.

Biofeedback-assisted relaxation is as effective as progressive muscle relaxation in reducing arousal in adults and this is also probably the case with children. Portable skin conductance biofeedback units are now widely avail-able for this purpose. However, biofeedback equipment increases the cost of treatment. It also does not provide opportunities for enhancing parent–adolescent relationships in the way that parent-assisted relaxation training does.

Interventions focusing on family relationships

Both preliminary assessment interviews and the results of self-monitoring tasks typically provide evidence that the adolescent's mood is influenced by family relationships, notably those characterized by confusing communi-cation, conflict, criticism, overinvolvement and triangulation (Asarnow *et al.*, 1993; Kaslow *et al.*, 1994; Mufson *et al.*, 1993; Oster and Caro, 1990). Furthermore, role relationship difficulties associated with family transitions, including the onset of adolescence, parental separation, bereavements and so forth, may contribute to depression. On the other hand, parental support, clear communication, non-conflictual approaches to solving relationship problems and clear roles tend to be associated with positive moods. The interventions that may be used to promote the types of family relationships that improve mood are:

➢ communication training;
➢ problem-solving training;
➢ facilitating support;
➢ renegotiating role relationships.

Communication training

Where depressed adolescents and their parents have difficulties communi-cating clearly with each other, communication training may be appropriate (Falloon *et al.*, 1993). A list of communication skills is given in Appendix 5. A common problem is that parents have difficulty listening to their youngsters and youngsters have difficulties clearly articulating their views to their parents. A second common communication problem is the difficulty parents have in listening to each other's views about how best to manage their adolescent's difficulties.

In some instances parents and children have never learned communication skills. In others, good communication skills have been acquired but intoxi-cation or intense emotions such as anger, anxiety or depression prevent parents and children from using these skills. Training in using communication skills is appropriate in the former situation, but in the latter the key problem to be solved is how to arrange episodes of communication that will be uninfluenced by intoxication or negative mood states. Communication skills may be artificially subdivided into those used for listening and those used for speaking. Parents and adolescents need, first, to be given an intellectual understanding of these skills. Then the clinician should model the skills for the clients. Clients should at this point be invited to try using the skills to discuss a neutral topic in the session. Let the episode of communication run for five or ten minutes and take notes of various difficulties that occur. Then give feedback and, in light of this, ask clients to complete the episode again. Typical mistakes include interrupting before the other person has finished, failing to summarize what the other person said accurately, attributing negative malicious intentions to the other person when they have not communicated that they hold such intentions, failing to check that the message was accurately sent, failing to check that the message has been accurately received, blaming and sulking.

Once clients can use the skills to exchange views on a neutral topic, they may then be used to exchange views on emotionally loaded issues, in the session first and later at home. Communication homework assignments should be highly specific, to prevent clients from lapsing into poor communication habits. Thus, specific members of a family should be invited to find out the other person's views on a specific topic. A time and place free of distractions should be agreed and a time limit of no more than 20 minutes set for initial communication assignments and 40 minutes when skills are better developed.

Problem-solving training

When it is apparent that depressed adolescents and their parents need to take a more systematic approach to resolving problems, problem-solving skills training is appropriate (Falloon *et al.*, 1993). A list of problem-solving skills is given in Appendix 6. Individual problem-solving training for depressed youngsters may be helpful when they have specific peer group or academic problems that they repeatedly fail to solve, such as joining in peer activities or managing homework assignments. As with communication difficulties, clients may have difficulties solving problems because they lack the skills or because intoxication, negative mood states or other factors interfere with the use of well developed skills. Where such factors are present, therapy should focus on removing these obstacles to effective problem-solving.

In problem-solving training, the sequence of stages described for communication training should be followed, with a progression from explanation of the skills listed in Appendix 6, to modelling, to rehearsal in the session with the focus on a neutral topic. Feedback should be given during rehearsal until the skills are well developed. Then clients may be invited to use the skills to solve emotionally laden problems.

When families are observed trying to solve emotionally laden problems, often the first pitfall they slide into is that of problem definition. Many clients need to be coached in how to translate a big, vague problem into a few small, specific problems. A second pitfall involves trying to solve more than one problem at a time. A third area of difficulty is helping clients to hold off on evaluating the pros and cons of any one solution until as many solutions as possible have been listed. This is often a particular difficulty in families with depressed members. This premature criticism of possible solutions creates a family culture within which no one ventures new ideas lest they be criticized. Family members require careful coaching in the skill of delaying evaluation of options until a large number have been generated. Without this, creative solutions to family problems that maintain the adolescent's depression may be more difficult to find. Often families need to be coached out of bad communication habits in problem-solving training, such as negative mind reading, where they attribute negative thoughts or feelings to others, blaming, sulking and abusing others. Where families with chronic problems successfully resolve a difficulty, a vital part of the coaching process is to help them celebrate this victory.

Facilitating support

Supportive conversations may be scheduled for time-limited periods, such as 30 minutes, at a set time each day. The role of the supporting family member is to use listening skills learned in the communications training exercise and do no more than summarize what the depressed adolescent has said and check that they have understood the adolescent correctly. No attempt should be made by the supporting family member to cheer up depressed adolescents or to make suggestions about how they might solve their problems. Family members may require coaching in this very difficult skill, since even the most patient parent or sibling will have urges to talk the adolescent out of the depression.

Renegotiating role relationships

Role relationship difficulties that maintain depression may be characterized by overinvolvement, criticism and problems associated with divided loyalties. What follows are some strategies for renegotiating these problematic role relationships.

Where parents have become overinvolved with their child and regularly engage in intrusive interactions, this non-supportive pattern may be disrupted by offering them the opportunity of having a break from caring for the depressed youngster by passing the responsibility over to the less involved parent. This type of intervention may be particularly useful in families where the overinvolved parent is inadvertently blocking the adolescent's completion of age-appropriate developmental tasks such as establishing autonomy and maintaining privacy. Often in such instances, the more the peripheral parent argues for the overinvolved parent to allow the adolescent some space, the more overintrusive the overinvolved parent becomes. This intervention of placing the peripheral parent in charge of the adolescent's welfare disrupts this pattern of triangulation.

Where one parent has become highly critical of the youngster and the depressive behaviour, the parent and adolescent may be encouraged to join forces to defeat or overcome the depression, which may be externalized and personified as a black knight, a dragon, a monster or some other mythological entity. The central feature of the intervention is that the parent and child join in a strong alliance against the depression, so the child feels supported by the parent. I have found this intervention particularly useful in families where one parent (typically the father) has become very critical of the child, while the other parent (typically the mother) sympathizes with the child's position.

In families where parents are separated or divorced, depressed adolescents often find the experience of divided loyalties very distressing. They feel that they must choose between being loyal to one parent or to the other, but either of these positions entails the loss of a relationship with a parent. This experience of divided loyalties is exacerbated when a parent expresses anger and disappointment concerning the ex-partner to the adolescent. In such instances, with coaching from the clinician, the adolescent may be helped to explain to the parents the extraordinary anguish that this type of triangulation causes and to ask the parents to make a commitment never to ask the teenager to take sides again, because the youngster is loyal to both parents and will remain so. Where adolescents have difficulty facing their parents and saying this, they may write them a letter containing these sentiments and read it out to them in the session. The parents, in reply, may be coached to agree to the adolescent's request. Where parents cannot consent to this, it is vital that they understand the consequences of this for the adolescent, namely chronic psychological problems, including depression.

Interventions focusing on cognition

The techniques described in this section are family-based variations of interventions developed for use with individual adults in cognitive therapy. Because any adolescent's belief systems will be inextricably bound up with

COLBY COMMUNITY COLLEGE LIBRARY

their parent's belief systems, I have found that this family-based approach to cognitive therapy is particularly useful with adolescents.

Interventions that focus on cognitions begin by teaching both parents and youngsters to identify automatic thoughts and their impact on mood. The adolescent and parents may be asked to give a current mood rating on a 10-point scale and then identify the thought they are telling themselves that accounts for that rating. A challenge may then be posed to the youngster, for example a difficult arithmetic problem or puzzle. After trying to solve the problem for a minute or so, the clinician may then ask the adolescent to give a mood rating and the automatic thought that underpins it. Usually, there will be a drop in mood associated with a negative thought arising from failure to solve the puzzle. In this way, the link between automatic thoughts and mood is established. It may be pointed out that the automatic thought (for example 'Because I can't do it quickly I'm stupid') could be replaced with another thought ('If I had a calculator I'd be finished now') that might lead to a less depressed mood rating.

The adolescent may be invited to keep track of automatic thoughts and related mood states using the self-monitoring system described earlier. Reviewing self-monitoring forms throws light on situations that lead to mood changes and the automatic thoughts that occur in these situations. Parents and adolescents may be helped to develop specific routines for challenging or neutralizing negative automatic thoughts. Three methods deserve particular mention:

➤ the CTR method;
➤ reattribution training;
➤ focusing on positives.

The CTR method – challenge, test, reward

Challenging negative automatic thoughts involves generating alternative self-statements that could have been made in a specific situation in which a negative automatic thought occurred and then looking for evidence to *test* the validity of these alternatives. Finally, when this task has been completed and the youngster has shown that the depressive automatic thought was invalid, he/she engages in self-*reward* or self-reinforcement (Beck, 1976; Kaslow and Rehm, 1991). So, for example, one alternative to the automatic thought 'He didn't talk to me so he doesn't like me' is 'He didn't talk to me because he is shy'. If there is evidence that the person in question never injured me before and on a couple of occasions smiled at me, then the more valid statement is that the person is shy. I may reward myself for challenging and testing this automatic thought by telling myself that I have done a good job of testing my automatic thought.

The CTR method may be taught within family sessions and the family may be asked to think about how much evidence there is for each of a series of negative automatic thoughts and possible alternatives. They may then be coached in praising themselves for testing the alternatives efficiently. Parents may be invited to prompt adolescents to use their CTR skills, in situations where low mood occurs.

Reattribution training

Challenging depressive attributions is a second strategy for reducing the impact of negative automatic thoughts (Abramson *et al.*, 1978). In particular failure situations that have led to negative automatic thoughts, the parents and the youngster are asked to rate the degree to which the negative automatic thought reflects an internal, global, stable attribution. For example, the automatic thought 'I couldn't do the problem because I've always been completely stupid' might receive the following ratings:

Internal Due to me	(1) 2 3 4 5 6 7 8 9 10	**External** Due to circumstances
Global To do with many situations	1 (2) 3 4 5 6 7 8 9 10	**Specific** To do with this situation
Stable Is permanent	(1) 2 3 4 5 6 7 8 9 10	**Unstable** Is temporary

An alternative self-statement, 'I couldn't do the problem because it's very hard and I'm having a bad day', might receive the following ratings, which characterize an optimistic rather than a pessimistic cognitive style:

Internal Due to me	1 2 3 4 5 6 7 8 9 (10)	**External** Due to circumstances
Global To do with many situations	1 2 3 4 5 6 7 8 (9) 10	**Specific** To do with this situation
Stable Is permanent	1 2 3 4 5 6 7 8 9 (10)	**Unstable** Is temporary

For each internal, global, stable explanation for failure, youngsters and their parents may be trained to ask whether alternative external, specific or unstable explanations may be offered that fit the available evidence.

Focusing on positives

Where adolescents selectively attend to negative aspects of their situation, and then criticize themselves, they and their parents may be shown how to complete mildly challenging activities and how to give a running commentary on how they are evaluating their performance and reinforcing themselves through the use of self-praise. They and their parents may then be invited to complete jointly this type of routine at home.

Training in social skills and problem-solving

Group activity programmes and a group therapy format may be used to help teenagers develop social skills so that they can initiate and maintain positive interactions with peers. Common problems with depressed teenagers include avoiding initiating conversations; engaging in self-critical or pessimistic talk that other teenagers find aversive; and withdrawing from complex social situations. These difficulties in turn lead to exclusion from peer group activities. Social skills training should aim to help youngsters learn strategies for tracking peer group conversations; identifying opportunities for contributing; and then making contributions to conversations and activities that benefit themselves and others. Youngsters may be coached in social skills by first being given a rationale for the skill; second observing a model of the appropriate skill; and then practising it and receiving verbal or videotaped corrective feedback and reinforcement.

A useful rationale is to explain that most peer groups want new members that are going to give something good (like companionship or good humour) rather than take something away (like replacing a good mood with a bad mood). When you are depressed, this takes some planning because the depression forces you to give nothing and take away any good mood there is. Coaching in social skills is a way of beating depression, by planning to give companionship and good humour rather than taking it away. In the long run, the use of social skills may help the youngster to get some friendships back.

Following this type of rationale, the clinician may show a videotape of an appropriate and inappropriate way of initiating a conversation or a conversation in which a youngster gives good humour or engages in depressive talk. In some of our groups I have taped clips from television programmes to use as models. In others, I and my colleagues modelled the interactions.

With rehearsal, youngsters are invited to imitate the behaviour demonstrated in the model. It is important that all approximations to positive social skills be praised and suggestions for improvement be made tactfully. Videotaped feedback, in my clinical experience, is useful only when significant improvement has been made that can clearly be pointed out to the youngster viewing the tape. If their performance is poor, the process of watching themselves engage in poor social skills on videotape may exacerbate their depression.

Once basic social skills such as joining, initiating and maintaining conversations have been mastered, training in social problem-solving may begin. Here, youngsters generate a list of difficult social situations that they fear, such as being criticized, snubbed, laughed at or embarrassed, and are asked to generate as many alternative ways of dealing with these problems as possible. Positive and negative possible outcomes of all these options may be explored and the group may then be coached in how to implement the most favourable solution. Again, video clips from soap operas and group members' favourite television programmes may be used to illustrate difficult peer group interactions and solutions to these interpersonal problems.

School interventions

Work with the school should help the child's teacher understand the formulation and develop supportive patterns of interaction with the child. Where children have become withdrawn, teachers may be helped to create opportunities where the depressed child can interact with peers.

Medication

The available evidence offers little support for the effectiveness of tricyclic antidepressant medication with depressed children, despite their unequivocal effectiveness with adults, but offers some support for the effectiveness of selective serotonin reuptake inhibitors (SSRIs) for the treatment of mood disorders in adolescents (Riddle *et al.*, 2001). There are therefore grounds for using SRRIs as an adjunct to psychosocial intervention. Prescription of antidepressants and the monitoring of side-effects are the responsibility of a physician (in most countries), who may share the care of a client with a counsellor, psychotherapist, clinical psychologist or other non-medical professional.

Management of parental mood problems

Interventions that focus on parental mood problems, a reduction of parental stress and the amplification of parental support should be prioritized if it is clear from the formulation that these factors will compromise the parent's capacity to help the adolescent recover. Many youngsters referred for treatment of adolescent depression come from families where one or both parents are depressed. In such instances, it is important to ensure that depressed parents are referred immediately for treatment, if they are to be able to engage effectively in family work to help their youngsters recover.

Where particular life stresses and support deficits such as marital conflict, conflict within the extended family, social isolation, inadequate accommodation, financial difficulties, work-related difficulties and so forth are severe enough to prevent any therapeutic progress, in a minority of instances it may be necessary to address these first. However, where possible, the focus of the work should be on helping the family to help the youngster to recover. Success with this goal may increase parental self-efficacy so that the parents are empowered to tackle their other life difficulties with greater confidence.

Managing relapse, disengagement and resistance

Depression is a recurrent disorder and while 90 per cent of episodes may resolve with intensive short-term intervention within 12 months, most children relapse. Therefore brief therapy, of the type described in this guide, must be offered within the context of a longer-term care programme. Children and parents may be trained to identify and cope with relapses and invited to recontact the service in the event of a further episode of depression. Each episode of contact may usefully be defined as time limited to a set number of sessions (e.g. 10 sessions). For each episode of contact, specific therapeutic goals may be set, such as reducing scores on the depression inventory included in Appendix 1 so that it falls below 18, or maintaining a mood score of 6 or more (on a 10-point scale) for 10 consecutive days.

The process of disengagement within a particular episode of contact begins once improvement is noticed. The interval between sessions is increased at this point. The degree to which the therapeutic goal of helping the youngster improve has been met is reviewed. Where goals have been achieved, the family's beliefs about the permanence of this change are clarified by asking questions such as:

> Do you believe that the improvements that have occurred recently are a flash in the pan or a real and lasting improvement?

Then the therapist helps the family construct an understanding of the change process by reviewing with them the problem, the formulation, their progress through the treatment programme and the concurrent improvement in the problem. Relapse management is also discussed (Marlatt and Gordon, 1985). Family members are helped to forecast the types of stressful situations in which relapses may occur; their probable negative reactions to relapses; and the ways in which they can use the lessons learned in therapy to cope with these relapses in a productive way. Disengagement is constructed as an episodic event rather than as the end of a relationship.

A central guideline for working with depressed adolescents is to set tasks where there is a very high chance of success. Thus psychoeducational input should be pitched at the youngster's ability level. Easy self-monitoring tasks should be given before progressing to more complex ones. Simple and small homework assignments focusing on activities, relationships and cognitions should be given first before moving on to more challenging invitations. Where youngsters have difficulty completing tasks, responsibility for this should be taken by the clinician, who probably asked more of the youngster and the family than they were ready for. It is very easy when working with depressed youngsters from families in which one of the parents is depressed to fall into a pattern of criticism and blaming the family for lack of progress. The challenge is to establish and maintain a good working alliance and find a pace of work that suits the family.

Part II: Attempted suicide

Depression is the psychological problem most commonly associated with suicide. In the US and the UK childhood suicide (for children under 14 years) is rare, with rates in the late 1980s being 0.8 and 0.7 per 100,000 respectively. On the other hand, teenage suicide is not a rare event and is on the increase, particularly among male teenagers. For 15–19-year-old males in the US and the UK in the late 1980s, the rates were 13.2 per 100,000 and 7.6 per 100,000, respectively (Shaffer and Piacentini, 1994). Parasuicide, or attempted suicide, is a common event. A mean parasuicide event rate of 195/100,000 per year was found in a World Health Organization 12-centre study covering much of Europe, and repetition of parasuicide was found to be common (Platt, 1992).

Risk and protective factors for suicide

Assessment of suicide risk is necessary:

➤ when youngsters have attempted suicide recently;
➤ when youngsters threaten self-harm;
➤ where there are signs of severe depression.

Suicide risk assessment involves assessing the degree to which a range of risk and protective factors are present in a particular case and making a judgement about the probability that a suicide attempt will be made. This is not an exact science. It involves careful interviewing and clinical judgement informed by what is known about risk and protective factors in suicide. In research on suicide, a distinction may be made between factors associated with completed suicide and those associated with parasuicide. Risk and protective factors for adolescent suicide are set out below and summarized in Table 3. Where appropriate, reference is made to factors associated with parasuicide.

Assessment of suicide risk should cover the following domains:

➤ suicidal ideation and intention;
➤ method lethality;
➤ precipitating factors;
➤ motivation;
➤ personality-based factors;
➤ disorder-related factors;

➤ historical factors;
➤ family factors;
➤ demographic factors.

The factors listed in Table 3 and discussed below are drawn from thorough literature reviews (Berman and Jobes, 1993; Brent, 1997; Cohen *et al.*, 1996; Group for the Advancement of Psychiatry, 1996; Jacobs, 1999; O'Connor and Sheehy, 2000; Rudd and Joiner, 1998; Shaffer and Piacentini, 1994; Zimmerman and Asnis, 1995).

Suicidal intention and ideation

Suicidal intention may be distinguished from suicidal ideation. Suicidal intention is characterized by:

➤ advanced planning;
➤ precautions against discovery;
➤ lethal method;
➤ absence of help-seeking;
➤ a final act.

Thus, when adolescents' attempted suicides are characterized by suicidal intention, there is evidence that they have engaged in advanced planning about taking their own lives and have taken precautions against discovery. There is also evidence that they have used a potentially lethal method, such as hanging, self-poisoning, using a gun or jumping from a very dangerous height, and have not sought help after making the suicide attempt. Youngsters with suicidal intentions typically have also completed a final act such as writing a suicide note. Where youngsters show all of these features of suicidal intention, there is a high risk of suicide.

With suicidal ideation, in contrast, adolescents report thinking about self-harm and possibly engaging in non-lethal self-harm such as superficial wrist-cutting but have no clear-cut plans to kill themselves. Suicidal intention and ideation probably reflect two ends of a continuum, with states that approximate suicidal intention reflecting a higher level of risk and those approximating suicidal ideation reflecting a lower level of risk.

The absence of suicidal intentions may be considered a protective factor. The acceptance by the adolescent of a verbal or written contract during a suicide risk assessment, not to attempt suicide, is also a protective factor. The commitment on the part of the parents of carers to monitor the adolescent constantly until all suicidal intention and ideation have abated is a further important protective factor to consider in this domain. This commitment may take the form of an oral or written contract between the clinician and the parents or carers.

Table 3. Risk and protective factors for suicide in adolescence

Risk factors	Domain	Protective factors
Suicidal intention Advanced planning Precautions against discovery Lethal method Absence of help-seeking A final act	**Suicidal intention and ideation**	Suicidal ideation (not intention) Acceptance by adolescent of no-suicide contract Acceptance by parents and carers of suicide monitoring
Availability of lethal method (guns and drugs)	**Method lethality**	Absence of lethal method
Loss of parents or partner by death, separation or illness Conflict with parents or partner Involvement in judicial system Severe personal illness Major examination failure Unwanted pregnancy Imitation of other suicides	**Precipitating factors**	Resolution of interpersonal conflict with parents or partner that precipitated suicide Acceptance and mourning of losses that precipitated suicide Physical and psychological distancing from peers or others who precipitated imitative suicide
Suicide attempted to serve the function of: • escaping an unbearable psychological state or situation • gaining revenge by inducing guilt • inflicting self-punishment • gaining care and attention • sacrificing the self for a greater good	**Motivation**	Capacity to develop non-destructive coping styles or engage in treatment to be better able to: • regulate difficult psychological states • modify painful situations • express anger assertively • resolve conflicts productively • mourn losses • manage perfectionistic expectations • solicit care and attention from others • cope with family disorganization

Factor category		
Personality-based factors	High level of hopelessness High level of perfectionism High level of impulsivity High levels of hostility and aggression Inflexible coping style	Low level of hopelessness Low level of perfectionism Low level of impulsivity Low levels of hostility and aggression Flexible coping style
Disorder-related factors	Depression Alcohol and drug abuse Conduct disorder Antisocial personality disorder Borderline personality disorder Epilepsy Chronic painful illness Multiple comorbid chronic disorders	Absence of psychological disorders Absence of physical disorders Absence of multiple comorbid chronic disorders Capacity to form therapeutic alliance and engage in treatment for psychological and physical disorders
Historical factors	Previous suicide attempts Loss of a parent in early life Previous psychiatric treatment Involvement in the juvenile justice system	No history of suicide attempts No history of loss of a parent in early life No history of psychiatric treatment No history of involvement in the juvenile justice system
Family factors	Family history of suicide attempts Family history of depression Family history of drug and alcohol abuse Family history of assaultive behaviour Disorganized unsupportive family Family deny seriousness of suicide attempts Family has high stress and crowding Family has low social support and is socially isolated	No family history of suicide attempts No family history of depression No family history of drug and alcohol abuse No family history of assaultive behaviour Well organized supportive family Family has low stress Family has high social support
Demographic factors	Male Social class 5 White (not black) in US Weak religious commitment Attempt made in early summer	Female Social classes 2, 3 or 4 Black (not white) in US Strong religious commitment

Method lethality

The lethality of the method used or threatened is an important factor to consider in assessing risk, with more lethal methods being associated with greater risk in some instances. Using a firearm, hanging, jumping from a great height and self-poisoning with highly toxic drugs are considered to be more lethal than cutting or overdosing on non-prescription drugs. Within this domain, the availability of a lethal method such as access to a firearm or highly toxic drugs constitutes an important risk factor for suicide. Self-harm, particularly superficially cutting the wrists and arms, should be distinguished from potentially lethal incomplete suicide attempts. Non-lethal self-harm of this sort is sometimes associated with an attempt to relieve tension or gain attention following an interpersonal crisis. This type of self-harming is sometimes preceded by a sense of emptiness or depersonalization (a sense of not being oneself). It is common among adolescents with a history of abuse or neglect and among adolescents with a history of repeated parasuicidal episodes.

However, the degree of suicidal intention cannot always be judged from the lethality of the method used. Where adolescents misunderstand the degree of lethality associated with a particular method, apparently minor parasuicidal gestures may be a significant risk factor for actual suicide.

The unavailability of lethal methods such as firearms and toxic drugs is an important protective factor. This protective factor can be put in place by inviting parents to remove guns, drugs and other lethal methods from the household or placing the adolescent in a place where there is no access to lethal methods.

Precipitating factors

Suicide attempts are commonly precipitated by interpersonal conflict or loss involving a parent or romantic attachment. Ongoing conflict with parents, particularly if this entails child abuse, is strongly associated with completed suicide. More severe abuse, combined physical and sexual abuse, and chronic abuse are all associated with higher risk. Conflict over disciplinary matters and rule-breaking, particularly if this involves a court appearance and imprisonment, are all associated with suicide attempts. For imprisoned adolescents, the risk of suicide attempts is greater during the early part of detention.

Loss of parents or a romantic partner through death, long-term separation, or severe chronic illness may precipitate attempted suicide. Other loss experiences such as diagnosis of severe personal illness (e.g. being HIV positive) or examination failure may precipitate self-harm. Adolescent pregnancy may also precipitate attempted suicide and may reflect a loss of innocence; it is also a potential focus for intense parent–adolescent conflict.

Suicide arising from imitation of others may be precipitated by suicides within the peer group, school or locality or media coverage of suicides.

Repeated suicide attempts are associated with impulsive separation following romantic relationship difficulties or recent court appearance associated with impulsive or aggressive antisocial behaviour.

Protective factors in this domain include the resolution of the interpersonal conflict with parents or romantic partner; acceptance and mourning of the losses that precipitated suicide; and physical and psychological distancing from peers or others who precipitated imitative suicide.

Motivation

Youngsters may be motivated to attempt suicide for a wide variety of reasons. Suicide is usually perceived by youngsters as the only feasible solution to a difficult problem involving interpersonal loss or conflict. In this respect, the act of suicide may be construed as fulfilling one or more functions, including:

➢ escaping an unbearable psychological state or situation;
➢ gaining revenge by inducing guilt;
➢ inflicting self-punishment;
➢ gaining care and attention;
➢ sacrificing the self for a greater good.

The potential for finding alternative ways of fulfilling the functions of attempted suicide is a protective factor. Thus flexibility about developing new coping styles for solving the problem for which the suicide attempt was a destructive solution places adolescents at lower risk for suicide.

Understanding suicidal motives and the functions that suicidal gestures are intended to fulfil is important in treatment planning. When the functions of an attempted suicide are understood, the treatment plan should help the youngster find other ways to fulfil these functions. That is, treatment plans should help youngsters: find less destructive ways of regulating difficult psychological states; modify painful situations; express anger assertively; resolve conflicts productively; mourn losses; manage perfectionistic expectations; solicit care and attention from others; and cope with family disorganization.

Personality-based factors

Personality traits that place adolescents at risk for suicide include hopelessness; perfectionism; impulsivity; hostility and aggression; and an inflexible coping style. Youngsters who attempt suicide view themselves as incapable of changing their situation and so the future, to them, looks hopeless. Perfectionism is a risk factor for suicide probably because it leads to heightened self-expectations, which may be difficult to achieve. Suicidal adolescents tend to be inflexible in their coping styles and have difficulties drawing on memories of successfully solving problems in the past and so have a limited repertoire of coping strategies to draw upon. Thus they resort to strategies that may be ineffective. Their aggression and impulsivity may lead them to engage in self-directed aggression with little reflection on other possible alternatives for solving their difficulties.

Low levels of personality traits that place adolescents at risk for suicide are protective factors in this domain, that is low levels of hopelessness; perfectionism; impulsivity; hostility and aggression. It has already been noted in the previous section that the potential for flexibility in finding alternatives to suicide as a way of coping is a protective factor also.

Disorder-related factors

The presence of depression is the single strongest health-related risk factor for future suicide. Depression is strongly associated with hopelessness, which paves the way for suicide. Major depression (a recurrent episodic mood disorder) is strongly associated with completed suicide, whereas dysthymia (a chronic, milder, non-episodic mood disorder) is associated with repeated suicide attempts. Other disorders that are risk factors for suicide include alcohol and drug abuse, conduct disorder, antisocial or borderline personality disorders. All of these are more common among impulsive individuals and impulsivity has been already been mentioned as personality-based risk factor for suicide. Epilepsy and chronic painful diseases are the two types of physical illness that place adolescents at increased risk of suicide. Increased suicide risk is strongly associated with multiple comorbid chronic psychological and physical disorders.

The absence of psychological or physical disorders and the absence of multiple comorbid chronic psychological and physical disorders are important protective factors in this domain. So too is the capacity to form a good therapeutic alliance and engage in a contract for treatment of the disorders.

Historical factors

A history of suicide attempts is the single strongest historical risk factor for future suicide. Other historical risk factors include loss of a parent in early life, previous psychiatric treatment and a history of involvement in the juvenile justice system. These three factors are particularly strongly associated with repeated suicidal attempts or parasuicide.

The absence of these historical events is a protective factor, as is a history of good premorbid adjustment.

Family factors

A family history of a range of problems – notably suicide attempts, depression, drug and alcohol abuse, and assaultive behaviour – places youngsters at risk for suicide. In addition, youngsters are placed at increased risk of suicide if their families are socially isolated, live in stressful, overcrowded conditions and if they deny the seriousness of the youngster's suicidal intentions or are unsupportive of the youngster.

A family history that does not entail suicide attempts, depression, drug and alcohol abuse, and assaultive behaviour is a protective factor. Where the family is well organized and supportive of the youngster and where there are low levels of stress and a high level of social support for the family as a whole, these may be considered as protective factors.

Demographic factors

Male adolescents are at greater risk for completed suicide, while female adolescents are at greatest risk of parasuicide. Males tend to use more lethal methods (guns and hanging) whereas females use less lethal methods (cutting or self-poisoning). Membership of social class 5 (unskilled workers with low incomes and educational levels) is a risk factor for completed suicide and repeated parasuicide, while membership of social class 1 (professional and higher managerial employees) is a risk factor for completed suicide only. In the US, suicide rates are higher for white than black adolescents. With respect to religion, adolescents from communities with lower levels of religious practice are at greater risk for suicide. With respect to seasonality, completed suicide is most common in early summer.

Protective demographic factors include being female; membership of social classes 2, 3 and 4; being black (not white) in the US; and having a strong commitment to religious values and practices.

Assessment of suicide risk

Family-focused interventions based on social learning theory for the management of suicide risk emphasize the importance of adopting a structured problem-solving approach that takes account of the adolescent's personal features and the social context within which the suicide attempt was made (Berman and Jobes,

1993; Brent, 1997; Cohen et al., 1996; Group for the Advancement of Psychiatry, 1996; Jacobs, 1999; Rudd and Joiner, 1998; Shaffer and Piacentini, 1994; Zimmerman and Asnis, 1995). The overriding objective of a consultation where suicide has been threatened or attempted is to prevent harm, injury or death.

Certain broad principles for assessment may be followed.

1. Offer immediate consultation.
2. Use the consultation process to develop a comprehensive understanding of the situation surrounding the suicide threat or attempt.
3. During the consultation, establish or deepen your working alliance with all significant members of the network.
4. Assess all of the risk and protective factors listed in Table 3. Check whether the factors were present in the past, the extent to which they were present during the recent episode, and whether they are immediately present. Where possible, obtain information relating to risk and protective factors from as many members of the network as possible. This includes the youngster who has threatened self-harm or attempted suicide, key members of the family, and previously involved professionals.
5. Identify people within the youngster's social network and the professional network who may be available to help implement a management plan.
6. Draw the information you obtain into a clear formulation on which a management plan can be based. The formulation must logically link together the risk factors identified in the case, to explain the occurrence of the episode of self-injurious behaviour and the current level of risk. It is important to specify predisposing factors and precipitating factors that led to an escalation from suicidal ideation to intention or from suicidal intention to self-injury. The management plan must specify the short-term action to be taken in the light of the formulation. The plan must logically indicate that the changes it entails will probably lower the risk of self-harm.

It is also vital that, until the risk of suicide has reduced, the youngster and the parents make a contract at the conclusion of each session to return to meet the clinician at a specified time. For the youngster, this contract involves making a commitment to not make further suicide attempts. For the parents or carers, the contract involves making a commitment to monitor the youngster so as to prevent further suicide attempts.

Family and multisystemic interviews

With adolescents it is useful to conduct at least three different interviews: one with the parents, guardians or foster parents alone; one with the child alone; and one whole-family interview. The separate parent and child interviews provide opportunities to obtain different perspectives on the presence or absence of risk and protective factors. The family interview may be used to explore differences between parent and child views of the situation and to observe patterns of whole-family interaction.

For example, in one case the parents reported that their child continually displayed attention-seeking behaviour and the self-injurious behaviour was just one more example of that. The child asserted that he felt neglected and occasionally abused by the parents and that his self-injurious behaviour was an attempt to escape from that abuse. Later, in a whole-family interview, the pattern of interaction that the parents and child engaged in was explored and the differences between their views of the situation were examined. This case also shows that with children and adolescents it is crucial to interview the child alone at some point during the evaluation. If the child's concerns are being discounted by the parents, they will be less inhibited in talking about them in a one-to-one situation. Also, if neglect or abuse is occurring, this can best be explored in an individual interview. Family interviews offer a forum within which parents can be invited to view suicidal behaviour and ideation as reflecting a broad contextual problem rather than a difficulty that is intrinsic to the child.

In custody and access cases, foster care cases, cases where a child is in a residential school or institution, key people involved in the child's network must all be interviewed, individually if necessary. These key people will include the person legally responsible for the child, the child's primary caretaker, the person most concerned that the referral be made, the teachers or care workers who see the child daily and other professionals who have been involved in case management, including social workers, paediatricians and the general practitioner.

Individual interview

When conducting the individual interview with the adolescent, it is important first to let the youngster know the duration of the interview and what will follow from it. If hospitalization or some other protective intervention is an option, it is better to mention that this is a possible outcome rather than to conceal it. It is also crucial to be accurate about the limits of confidentiality. You must let the youngster know that you will not break a confidence that they ask you to keep unless it is necessary for ensuring their safety. Initially, to establish rapport, it may be useful to start by asking about some relatively unthreatening area, like schoolwork or friendships. Once you have established a working relationship with the youngster, move on to the central part of the interview.

In cases where a suicide attempt has been made, obtain a detailed description of the self-destructive behaviour that led to the referral and all related suicidal ideation and intentions. Specifically note whether the behaviour was dangerous and the strength of the child's will to die. Note the presence of a detailed plan, the taking of precautions to avoid discovery and the carrying out of a final act, such as making a will or writing a note. If you are reassessing a youngster who has been hospitalized with a view to discharging the case, or if you are assessing a case where suicide is suspected but no self-injurious behaviour has occurred, ask these questions:

➤ Have you thought of harming yourself?
➤ How strong is the urge to harm yourself?
➤ Have you a plan to harm yourself?
➤ What preparations have you made to harm yourself?
➤ What method do you expect you will use to harm yourself?
➤ Will you let others know about your plan to harm yourself or will it be secretive?
➤ Will you write a letter to anyone explaining why you are harming yourself?
➤ Suppose, you harmed yourself and died, what do you hope your family/ your mum/your dad/your brother/your sister would think/do/feel?
➤ Suppose, you harmed yourself but didn't die, what do you hope your family/your mum/your dad/your brother/your sister would think/do/feel?

Note whether the plan includes specific details of a dangerous method. The Beck Scale for Suicide Ideation (Beck and Steer, 1991) is a useful adjunct to a clinical interview, especially where youngsters are reluctant to talk. Invitations to engage in writing, drawing or painting offer other avenues for understanding youngsters' world views, especially where they are particularly reluctant to engage in conversation.

In cases where an attempt has been made, build up a picture of the immediate circumstances surrounding the episode. Clarify whether this is an escalation of an entrenched pattern of interaction around previous suicidal ideas or intentions. In cases where no self-injury has occurred but where suicidal ideation is present, ask the youngster to describe the sequence of events that led up to and followed on from episodes of suicidal ideation.

Identify the youngster's perception of the network and their perception of the roles of significant people in the recent episode and previous episodes of suicidal ideation or self-injurious behaviour. The aim here is to obtain a coherent account of how the youngster came to view his/her life situation as hopeless and selected self-harm as a solution to this experience of hopelessness. Include a full discussion of the youngster's family, friends and involved professionals in this assessment. It is vital to take account of risk and protective factors that may have been included in the sequence of events that led to the child experiencing hopelessness and attempting or considering suicide. Here are some questions that may be useful in eliciting information about the risk and protective factors listed in Table 3. All of these questions should be followed up with probes and linked together with alliance-building reassurance.

- ➢ Can you tell me about the things that were happening before you tried to (threatened to) harm yourself?
- ➢ What was going wrong in your life?
- ➢ How did you reach the decision to end your life?
- ➢ How exactly did you harm yourself?
- ➢ What happened afterwards and how did you survive?
- ➢ In what way did you believe that ending your life would solve the difficulties you faced?
- ➢ When you look back on that episode, do you think now that there were other things you could have done, besides harming yourself, to deal with the difficulties you faced?
- ➢ When you look into the future now, are you hopeful about changing your situation so that it will become more bearable?
- ➢ To what extent do you think that the high expectations that you have of yourself may push you towards self-harm again?
- ➢ To what extent do you think that you acted on impulse, without thinking, when you harmed yourself?
- ➢ Do you expect that you may act on impulse, without thinking, and harm yourself again?
- ➢ Have you had problems with low mood in the past?
- ➢ Have you tried to harm yourself before?
- ➢ Can you tell me about that episode, how it started, what happened, how it ended?
- ➢ Have you been in trouble at school or with the courts because of rule-breaking in the past?
- ➢ Have you been using drugs or alcohol much in the past?
- ➢ Have you attended a clinic for help with any problems like low mood, being in trouble, or using drugs or alcohol in the past?
- ➢ Have you been treated for any painful health problems or illnesses?
- ➢ Are you on medication for any conditions such as epilepsy?
- ➢ Has anyone in your family had problems with low mood, getting in trouble with the law or using too much drugs or alcohol?
- ➢ In your family, is there anyone you can turn to now for help with the difficulties you face?

Information from the interview may be supplemented with information from the questionnaires for assessing mood, family life and life stresses contained in Appendices 1, 7 and 8. At the conclusion of the interview, integrate the adolescent's story, check its accuracy and agree a plan for discussing this account with parents or carers and significant members of the adolescent's network.

Management of suicide risk

The principal focused interventions in cases of suicide risk are home-based care or referral for hospital-based or residential care.

Home-based care

With home-based care, the clinician and other relevant team members make a no-suicide contract with the adolescent and a monitoring contract with the parents or carers.

No-suicide contract

The no-suicide contract is an agreement, either oral or written, between the adolescent and clinician not to attempt suicide before the next appointment. The contract should also include the steps that the adolescent should take if the circumstances that triggered the previous suicidal threat or attempt recur or if suicidal intentions develop. Such steps may include disengaging from conflict with parents, partners, peers or others; avoiding catastrophizing about loss experiences; engaging in supportive conversation with a parent or carer; engaging in a distracting or soothing activity such as reading or listening to restful music; and telephoning the clinic's 24-hour on-call service as a last resort if strong suicidal ideation and intentions persist.

Monitoring contract

The parents or carers are invited to agree to a monitoring contract. This entails developing a family rota for keeping the youngster under 24-hour supervision to prevent a suicide attempt; agreeing that the person on the rota will engage only in supportive and non-conflictual conversation with the youngster; and telephoning the clinic's 24-hour on-call service as a last resort if strong suicidal ideation and intentions persist.

The 24-hour on-call service

Ideally, the no-suicide and monitoring contract are offered as part of thera-peutic plan in which the adolescent and parents are given a 24-hour on-call telephone number to contact a member of the treatment team if strong suicidal ideation and intentions persist. This has been shown significantly to reduce the number of suicide attempts and threats (Brent, 1997).

Treatment plan

The no-suicide and monitoring contract are offered as part of therapeutic plan that involves the adolescent and parents being invited to attend a series of sessions aimed at planning ways to modify risk or precipitating factors that contributed to the suicide attempt or threat. The treatment plan should address the functions of an attempted suicide and help the youngster in collaboration with the parents. It should also aim to treat the underlying depression and related difficulties, such as conduct problems and drug abuse. The treatment pro-gramme described for depression in Part I of this guide is appropriate here.

Active follow-up

Adolescents who attempt or threaten suicide are at risk for not attending follow-up appointments and so an active approach to follow-up is a vital part of the no-suicide contract and the parents' monitoring contract. The adol-escent and parents should be given a definite appointment after the initial consultation and this should be within a couple of days of the first meeting. The family should be contacted by telephone to remind them about the appointment and to enquire about non-attendance if this occurs. The number, duration and agenda for therapeutic sessions should be made clear to both the parents and the adolescent from the outset and the importance of follow-up to prevent further suicide threats and attempt should be highlighted.

Hospital-based care

With hospital-based and residential care, while the client is actively suicidal, 24-hour constant observation should be arranged in consultation with nurs-ing or residential care staff. As part of the admission contract, the parents or legal guardians should be invited to attend a series of sessions aimed at planning ways to modify risk or precipitating factors that contributed to the crisis and which, when modified, would create a safe context for discharge from hospital or residential care unit. Thereafter, the protocol outlined above for home-based care should be followed.

References

Abramson, L., Seligman, M. and Teasdale, J. (1978). Learned helplessness in humans: critique and reformulation. *Journal of Abnormal Psychology*, *87*, 49–74.

American Psychiatric Association (1994). *Diagnostic and Statistical Manual of Mental Disorders* (4th edn) (DSM–IV). Washington, DC: APA.

Asarnow, J., Goldstein, M., Thompson, M. and Guthrie, D. (1993). One-year outcomes of depressive disorders in child psychiatric in-patients: evaluation of the prognostic power of a brief measure of expressed emotion. *Journal of Child Psychology and Psychiatry*, *34*, 129–137.

Bateman, A., Brown, D. and Peddar, J. (2000). *Introduction to Psychotherapy. An Outline of Psychodynamic Principles and Practice.* London: Routledge.

Beck, A. (1976). *Cognitive Therapy and the Emotional Disorders.* New York: International Universities Press.

Beck, A. and Steer, R. (1991). *Beck Scale for Suicide Ideation.* New York: Psychological Corporation.

Berman, A. and Jobes, D. (1993). *Adolescent Suicide: Assessment and Intervention.* Washington, DC: APA.

Birleson, P. (1981). The validity of depressive disorder in childhood and the development of a self-rating scale: a research report. *Journal of Child Psychology and Psychiatry*, *22*, 73–88.

Birleson, P., Hudson, I., Buchanan, D. and Wolff, S. (1987). Clinical evaluation of a self-rating scale for depressive disorder in childhood (Depression Self-Rating Scale). *Journal of Child Psychology and Psychiatry*, *28*, 43–60.

Brent, D. (1997). The aftercare of adolescents with deliberate self-harm. *Journal of Child Psychology and Psychiatry*, *38*, 277–286.

Carr, A. (1999). *Handbook of Clinical Child Psychology: A Contextual Approach.* London: Routledge.

Carr, A. (2000). *Family Therapy: Concepts, Process and Practice.* Chichester: Wiley.

Cohen, P., Cohen, J., Kasen, S., Velez, C., Hartmark, C., Johnson, J., Rojas, M., Brook, J. and Streuning, E. (1993). An epidemiological study of disorders in late childhood and adolescence – 1. Age- and gender-specific prevalence. *Journal of Child Psychology and Psychiatry*, *34*, 851–867.

Cohen, Y., Spirito, A. and Brown, L. (1996). Suicide and suicidal behaviour. In R. DiClemente, W. Hansen and L. Ponton (Eds.) *Handbook of Adolescent Health Risk Behaviour* (pp.193–224). New York: Plenum.

Epstein, N., Baldwin, L. and Bishop, D. (1983). The McMaster Family Assessment Device. *Journal of Marital and Family Therapy*, *9*, 171–180.

Falloon, I., Laporta, M., Fadden, G. and Graham-Hole, V. (1993). *Managing Stress in Families.* London: Routledge.

Farmer, A. and McGuffin, P. (1989). The classification of depressions: contemporary confusions revisited. *British Journal of Psychiatry*, *155*, 437–443.

Group for the Advancement of Psychiatry (1996). *Adolescent Suicide.* Report No. 140. Washington, DC: APA.

Harrington, R. (1993). *Depressive Disorder in Childhood and Adolescence.* Chichester: Wiley.

Jacobs, D. (Ed.) (1999). *The Harvard Medical School Guide to Suicide Assessment and Intervention.* San Francisco: Jossey Bass.

Kaslow, N., Deering, C. and Racusin, G. (1994). Depressed children and their families. *Clinical Psychology Review*, *14*, 39–59.

Kaslow, N. and Rehm, L. (1991). Childhood depression. In T. Kratochwill and R. Morris (Eds.) *The Practice of Child Therapy* (pp. 73–45). New York: Pergamon.

Kazdin, A., French, N. Unis, A., Esveldt-Dawson, K. and Sherick, R. (1983). Hopelessness, depression and suicidal intent among psychiatrically disturbed inpatient children. *Journal of Consulting and Clinical Psychology*, *51*, 504–510.

Kovacs, M. (1997). The Emanuel Miller Memorial Lecture 1994. Depressive disorders in childhood: an impressionistic landscape. *Journal of Child Psychology and Psychiatry*, *38*, 287–298.

Kovacs, M. and Beck, A. (1977). An empirical clinical approach towards definition of childhood depression. In J. Schulterbrandt *et al.* (Eds.) *Depression in Children* (pp. 1–25). New York: Raven.

Lewinsohn, P., Clarke, G. and Rohde, P. (1994). Psychological approaches to the treatment of depression in adolescents. In H. Reynolds and F. Johnson (Eds.) *Handbook of Depression in Children and Adolescents* (pp. 309–344). New York: Plenum.

Marlatt, G. and Gordon, J. (1985). *Relapse Prevention.* New York: Guilford.

Mufson, L., Moreau, D., Weissman, M. and Klerman, G. (1993). *Interpersonal Psychotherapy for Depressed Adolescents.* New York: Guilford.

O'Connor, R. and Sheehy, N. (2000). *Understanding Suicidal Behaviour.* Leicester: BPS Books.

Oster, G. and Caro, J. (1990). *Understanding and Treating Depressed Adolescents and Their Families.* New York: Wiley.

Platt, S. (1992). Parasuicide in Europe. The WHO/EURO multicentre study on parasuicide. *Acta Psychiatrica Scandanavica, 85,* 97–104.

Reynolds, H. and Johnson, F. (1994). *Handbook of Depression in Children and Adolescents.* New York: Plenum.

Riddle, M., Kastelic, E. and Frosch, E. (2001). Pediatric psychopharmacology. *Journal of Child Psychology and Psychiatry, 42,* 73–90.

Rudd, M. and Joiner, T. (1998). The assessment, management and treatment of suicidality: towards clinically informed and balanced standards of care. *Clinical Psychology: Science and Practice, 5,* 135–150.

Shaffer, D. and Piacentini, J. (1994). Suicide and attempted suicide. In M. Rutter, E. Taylor and L. Hersov (Eds.) *Child and Adolescent Psychiatry: Modern Approaches* (3rd edn, pp. 407–424). Oxford: Blackwell.

Stark, K. and Kendall, P. (1996). *Treating Depressed Children: Therapists' Manual for ACTION.* Ardmore, PA: Workbook Publishing.

Williams, J. (1992). *The Psychological Treatment of Depression. A Guide to the Theory and Practice of Cognitive Behaviour Therapy* (2nd edn). London: Routledge.

Wood, A., Harrington, R. and Moore, A. (1996). Controlled trial of a brief cognitive–behavioural intervention in adolescent patients with depressive disorders. *Journal of Child Psychology and Psychiatry, 37,* 737–746.

World Health Organization (1996). *Multiaxial Classification of Child and Adolescent Psychiatric Disorders: ICD–10.* Geneva: WHO.

Zimmerman, J. and Asnis, G. (Eds.) (1995). *Treatment Approaches with Suicidal Adolescents.* New York: Wiley.

Further reading

For clients

Stark, K., Kendall, P., McCarthy, M., Stafford, M., Barron, R. and Thomeer, M. (1996). *A Workbook for Overcoming Depression.* Ardmore, PA: Workbook Publishing.

Assessment

Battle, J. (1992). *Culture-Free Self-Esteem Inventories. Examiner's Manual.* Austin, TS: Pro-ed.

Beck, A. and Steer, R. (1991). *Beck Scale for Suicide Ideation.* New York: Psychological Corporation.

Kovacs, M. and Beck, A. (1977). An empirical clinical approach towards definition of childhood depression. In J. Schulterbrandt *et al.* (Eds.) *Depression in Children* (pp. 1–25). New York: Raven.

Treatment manuals and resources

Berman, A. and Jobes, D. (1993). *Adolescent Suicide: Assessment and Intervention.* Washington, DC: APA.

Clarke, G., Lewinsohn, P. and Hops, H. (2000). *Leader's Manual for Adolescent Groups. Adolescent Coping with Depression Course.* Portland, OR: Center for Health Research. http://www.kpchr.org/.

Jacobs, D. (Ed.) (1999). *The Harvard Medical School Guide to Suicide Assessment and Intervention.* San Francisco: Jossey Bass.

Mufson, L., Moreau, D., Weissman, M. and Klerman, G. (1993). *Interpersonal Psychotherapy for Depressed Adolescents.* New York: Guilford.

Oster, G. and Caro, J. (1990). *Understanding and Treating Depressed Adolescents and Their Families.* New York: Wiley.

Stark, K. and Kendall, P. (1996). *Treating Depressed Children: Therapists' Manual for ACTION.* Ardmore, PA: Workbook Publishing.

Appendices

Appendix 1. Mood Scale

Please circle the answer that applies to you for each statement and answer as honestly as you can. The statements refer to how *you* have felt *over the past week*. There are no right answers. It is important to say how you have felt. Thank you.

1. I look forward to things as much as I used to

Most times	Sometimes	Never
0	1	2

2. I sleep very well

Most times	Sometimes	Never
0	1	2

3. I feel like crying

Most times	Sometimes	Never
2	1	0

4. I like to go out playing

Most times	Sometimes	Never
0	1	2

5. I feel like running away

Most times	Sometimes	Never
2	1	0

6. I get tummy aches

Most times	Sometimes	Never
2	1	0

7. I have lots of energy

Most times	Sometimes	Never
0	1	2

8. I enjoy my food

Most times	Sometimes	Never
0	1	2

9. I can stick up for myself

Most times	Sometimes	Never
0	1	2

10. I think life isn't worth living

Most times	Sometimes	Never
2	1	0

11. I am good at things I do

Most times	Sometimes	Never
0	1	2

12. I enjoy the things I do as much as I used to

Most times	Sometimes	Never
0	1	2

13. I like talking with my family

Most times	Sometimes	Never
0	1	2

14. I have horrible dreams

Most times	Sometimes	Never
2	1	0

15. I feel very lonely

Most times	Sometimes	Never
2	1	0

16. I am easily cheered up

Most times	Sometimes	Never
0	1	2

17. I feel so sad I can hardly stand it

Most times	Sometimes	Never
2	1	0

18. I feel very bored

Most times	Sometimes	Never
2	1	0

Adapted from Birleson's (1981; Birleson *et al.*, 1987) Depression Self-Rating Scale. The clinician should add circled scores together to obtain a score between 0 and 36. Scores above 18 suggest low mood. Scores above 27 suggest very low mood.

Appendix 2. What is depression?
Notes for young people and their parents

Depression is a complex condition involving changes in mood, biological functioning, thinking, behaviour and relationships.

Vulnerability to depression may be due to genetic factors or early experiences of loss. Current episodes of depression arise from a build-up of recent life stress, which activates the vulnerability. The life stress is then maintained by depressed thinking, action and relationships.

Genetic vulnerability may be understood as a nervous system that *goes slow* under pressure and disrupts sleep, appetite and energy. This going slow leads to depressed mood. Early loss-related vulnerability is a set of memories about loss that have been filed away in the mind, but are taken out when a recent loss occurs. The files inform the youngster that more and more losses will occur and this leads to depressed mood.

Overcoming depression involves learning how to control and change patterns of thinking, action and relationships that maintain depression. Thinking processes, or beliefs, behavioural routines and ways of managing relationships that maintain depressed mood are under conscious control, so treatment focuses on learning to change these three things.

The role of the family is to help the youngster develop new beliefs, routines and ways of managing relationships that protect him or her from becoming stuck in low moods. In treating depression, the youngster and the family are a problem-solving team. The clinician is the coach.

A diagram of this explanation of depression is presented below. Somatic state has also been included in the diagram. Antidepressant medication (selective serotonin reuptake inhibitors or SSRIs) may be used to regulate sleep and appetite and increase energy levels.

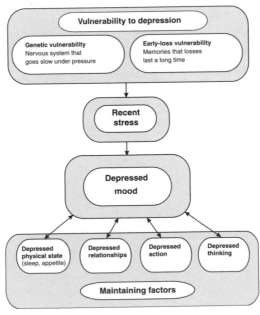

Appendix 3. Self-monitoring form for low mood

When you have finished dealing with a situation that changed your mood, fill out one line of the form overleaf. This will help you to keep track of:

➤ the types of situations in which your mood changes;
➤ what you think about in those situations;
➤ how these thoughts and situations affect your mood;
➤ how you cope with these thoughts and situations;
➤ how your coping strategies improve your mood.

Day and time	What happened before your mood changed?	Give a rating for your mood before it changed (1 = low; 10 = high)	What negative things were you thinking as your mood changed?	Give a rating for your mood after it changed (1 = low; 10 = high)	What positive coping responses did you use? (CTR, relaxation, leave situation, get support, other)	Give a rating for your mood after it changed (1 = low; 10 = high)

Appendix 4. Relaxation exercises

After a couple of weeks of daily practice, you will have developed enough skill to use these exercises to get rid of unwanted body tension.

➤ Set aside 20 minutes a day to do these relaxation exercises.

➤ Do them at the same time and in the same place every day.

➤ Before you begin, remove all distractions (by turning off bright lights, the radio, etc.) and loosen any tight clothes (like belts, ties or shoes).

➤ Lie on a bed or recline in a comfortable chair with the eyes lightly closed.

➤ Before and after each exercise breathe in deeply and exhale slowly three times while saying the word 'relax'.

➤ Repeat each exercise twice.

➤ Throughout the exercises, if your parent is helping you, ask them to speak in a calm, relaxed, quiet voice.

Area	Exercise
Hands	Close your hands into fists. Then allow them to open slowly. Notice the change from tension to relaxation in your hands and allow this change to continue further and further still so the muscles of your hands become more and more relaxed.
Arms	Bend your arms at the elbow and touch your shoulders with your hands. Then allow them to return to the resting position. Notice the change from tension to relaxation in your arms and allow this change to continue further and further still so the muscles of your arms become more and more relaxed.
Shoulders	Hunch your shoulders up to your ears. Then allow them to return to the resting position. Notice the change from tension to relaxation in your shoulders and allow this change to continue further and further still so the muscles of your shoulders become more and more relaxed.
Legs	Point your toes downwards. Then allow them to return to the resting position. Notice the change from tension to relaxation in the fronts of your legs and allow this change to continue further and further still so the muscles in the fronts of your legs become more and more relaxed. Point your toes upwards. Then allow them to return to the resting position. Notice the change from tension to relaxation in the backs of your legs and allow this change to continue further and further still so the muscles in the backs of your legs become more and more relaxed.
Stomach	Take a deep breath and hold it for three seconds, tensing the muscles in your stomach as you do so. Then breathe out slowly.

Notice the change from tension to relaxation in your stomach muscles and allow this change to continue further and further still so your stomach muscles become more and more relaxed.

Face

Clench your teeth tightly together. Then relax. Notice the change from tension to relaxation in your jaw and allow this change to continue further and further still so the muscles in your jaw become more and more relaxed.

Wrinkle your nose up. Then relax. Notice the change from tension to relaxation in the muscles around the front of your face and allow this change to continue further and further still so the muscles of your face become more and more relaxed.

Shut your eyes tightly. Then relax. Notice the change from tension to relaxation in the muscles around your eyes and allow this change to continue further and further still so the muscles around your eyes become more and more relaxed.

All over

Now that you've done all your muscle exercises, check that all areas of your body are as relaxed as can be. Think of your hands and allow them to relax a little more.

Think of your arms and allow them to relax a little more.

Think of your shoulders and allow them to relax a little more.

Think of your legs and allow them to relax a little more.

Think of your stomach and allow it to relax a little more.

Think of your face and allow it to relax a little more.

Breathing

Breathe in ... one ... two ... three ... and out slowly ... one ... two ... three ... four ... five ... six ... and again.

Breathe in ... one ... two ... three ... and out slowly ... one ... two ... three ... four ... five ... six ... and again.

Breathe in ... one ... two ... three ... and out slowly ... one ... two ... three ... four ... five ... six ....

Visualizing

Imagine you are lying on beautiful sandy beach and you feel the sun warm your body.

Make a picture in your mind of the golden sand and the warm sun.

As the sun warms your body you feel more and more relaxed.

As the sun warms your body you feel more and more relaxed.

As the sun warms your body you feel more and more relaxed.

The sky is a clear, clear blue. Above you, you can see a small white cloud drifting away into the distance.

As it drifts away you feel more and more relaxed.

It is drifting away and you feel more and more relaxed.

It is drifting away and you feel more and more relaxed.

As the sun warms your body you feel more and more relaxed.

As the cloud drifts away you feel more and more relaxed.

(Wait for 30 seconds.)

When you are ready, open your eyes ready to face the rest of the day relaxed and calm.

Appendix 5. Guidelines for listening and communications skills

Specific guidelines

Listening skills
- Listen without interruption
- Summarize key points
- Check that you have understood accurately
- Reply

Communication skills
- Decide on specific key points
- Organize them logically
- Say them clearly
- Check you have been understood
- Allow space for a reply the other person

General guidelines

- Make a time and place for clear communication
- Remove distractions and turn off the television
- Discuss one problem at a time
- Try to listen with the intention of accurately remembering what was said
- Try to listen without judging what is being said
- Avoid negative mind-reading
- State your points without attacking
- Avoid blaming, sulking or abusing
- Avoid interruptions
- Take turns fairly
- Be brief
- Make congruent 'I' statements

Appendix 6. Guidelines for problem-solving skills

Specific guidelines

- Define the problem
- Brainstorm options
- Explore pros and cons
- Agree on a joint action plan
- Implement the plan
- Review progress
- Revise the original plan

General guidelines

- Make a time and place for clear communication
- Remove distractions and turn off the television
- Discuss one problem at a time
- Divide one big problem into a few small problems
- Tackle problems one at a time
- Avoid vague problem definitions
- Define problems briefly
- Show that the problem (not the person) makes you feel bad
- Acknowledge your share of the responsibility in causing the problem
- Do not explore pros and cons until you have finished brainstorming
- Celebrate success

Appendix 7. Family Life Scale

Please circle the answer that applies to the way you see your family for each statement. Answer as honestly as you can. The statements refer to how *you* have seen your family **over the past week.** There are no right answers. It is important to say how you have seen your family. Thank you.

1. Planning family activities is difficult because we misunderstand each other

Strongly agree	Agree	Disagree	Strongly disagree
3	2	1	0

2. In times of crisis we can turn to each other for support

Strongly agree	Agree	Disagree	Strongly disagree
0	1	2	3

3. We cannot talk to each other about the sadness we feel

Strongly agree	Agree	Disagree	Strongly disagree
3	2	1	0

4. Individuals are accepted for what they are

Strongly agree	Agree	Disagree	Strongly disagree
0	1	2	3

5. We avoid discussing our fears and concerns

Strongly agree	Agree	Disagree	Strongly disagree
3	2	1	0

6. We can express feelings to each other

Strongly agree	Agree	Disagree	Strongly disagree
0	1	2	3

7. There are lots of bad feelings in the family

Strongly agree	Agree	Disagree	Strongly disagree
3	2	1	0

8. We feel accepted for what we are

Strongly agree	Agree	Disagree	Strongly disagree
0	1	2	3

9. Making decisions is a problem for our family

Strongly agree	Agree	Disagree	Strongly disagree
3	2	1	0

10. We are able to make decisions about how to solve problems

Strongly agree	Agree	Disagree	Strongly disagree
0	1	2	3

11. We don't get along well together

Strongly agree	Agree	Disagree	Strongly disagree
3	2	1	0

12. We confide in each other

Strongly agree	Agree	Disagree	Strongly disagree
0	1	2	3

The clinician should add circled scores together to obtain a score between 0 and 36. Scores above 18 suggest that the respondent perceives significant family difficulties. Scores above 24 suggests respondent perceives extreme family difficulties.
Adapted from Epstein *et al*. (1983) McMaster Family Assessment Device.

Appendix 8. Life Stress Questionnaire

Please circle the answer that applies to you for each statement and answer as honestly as you can.
There are no right answers.
It is important to indicate the life stresses that you have faced.
Thank you.

This list of 28 statements refers to events that have happened in the past six months

1.	I have been had very serious arguments with my parents	Yes	No
2.	I have had a serious argument with my closest boyfriend or girlfriend	Yes	No
3.	I have moved house	Yes	No
4.	I have changed schools	Yes	No
5.	I have been bullied	Yes	No
6.	I have had serious money difficulties	Yes	No
7.	I have had serious drug or alcohol problems	Yes	No
8.	I (or my girlfriend) have become pregnant by mistake	Yes	No
9.	I have failed (or believe I will fail) an important exam	Yes	No
10.	I have been in serious trouble at school	Yes	No
11.	I have been in serious trouble with the police	Yes	No
12.	My parents have separated from each other	Yes	No
13.	I have been separated from my parents	Yes	No
14.	My closest girlfriend or boyfriend has left me	Yes	No
15.	One of my parents has become extremely ill	Yes	No
16.	I have become extremely ill	Yes	No
17.	My closest girlfriend or boyfriend has become extremely ill	Yes	No
18.	One of my parents has died	Yes	No
19.	My closest girlfriend or boyfriend has died	Yes	No
20.	Some people I know (or have seen) have recently killed themselves	Yes	No

21.	I have been feeling like too much is expected of me	Yes	No
22.	I have been acting on impulse without thinking and hurt myself	Yes	No
23.	I have been acting on impulse without thinking and hurt others	Yes	No
24.	I have thought of harming or killing myself	Yes	No
25.	I have made definite plans to harm or kill myself	Yes	No
26.	I have actually tried to harm or kill myself	Yes	No
27.	I have tried to kill myself and made sure no one would get to me before I was dead	Yes	No
28.	I have written a letter to my family or friends explaining why I tried to kill myself	Yes	No

These 12 statements refer to events that have happened at any time during your life

1.	I had treatment for depression or bad nerves	Yes	No
2.	I have had serious drug or alcohol problems	Yes	No
3.	I have been in serious trouble for fighting, stealing or rule-breaking	Yes	No
4.	I have been to court for breaking the law	Yes	No
5.	I have has a long-term painful illness	Yes	No
6.	I have epilepsy or a seizure disorder or fits	Yes	No
7.	One of my parents died when I was young	Yes	No
8.	One of my parents had depression or bad nerves	Yes	No
9.	One of my parents had alcohol or drug problems	Yes	No
10.	One of my parents was in court for breaking the law	Yes	No
11.	In the past I have tried to harm myself	Yes	No
12.	In the past one of my parents has tried to harm themselves	Yes	No